JUDAISM

Volumes in the Religious Traditions of the World Series

Edited by H. Byron Earhart

Religions of Japan *by H. Byron Earhart*
Religions of China *by Daniel L. Overmyer*
Hinduism *by David M. Knipe*
Buddhism *by Robert C. Lester*
Christianity *by Sandra S. Frankiel*
Judaism *by Michael Fishbane*
Islam *by Frederick Denny*
Religions of Africa *by E. Thomas Lawson*
Native Religions of North America *by Åke Hultkrantz*
Religions of Mesoamerica *by David Carrasco*

JUDAISM

Revelation
and Traditions

MICHAEL FISHBANE

HarperSanFrancisco
A Division of HarperCollins*Publishers*

Designed by Donna Davis

Library of Congress Cataloging in Publication Data

Fishbane, Michael A.

 Judaism: revelation and traditions.

 (Religious traditions of the world)

  Bibliography: p.
  1. Judaism. I. Title. II. Series.
BM561.F49   1987   296   85-42775
ISBN 0-06-062655-0

99 00 01   RRD   20 19 18 17 16

For my mother,
with love

Contents

Editor's Foreword   ix

Preface   1

Chronology of Jewish Religious History   3

Chapter I. Introduction   11

Chapter II. Judaism as an Ideological System   25

    Rabbinic Patterns of This-Worldly Holiness and Salvation   26

    Rabbinic Patterns of Hidden Meanings and Otherworldly Concerns   63

    The Modern Period   76

Chapter III. Judaism as a Ritual System   83

    The Calendrical Cycle of Holiness   85

    The Life Cycle of Holiness   101

    The Social Circles of Holiness   108

Chapter IV. Jews and Judaism in Modern Times   114

    A Tale of Two Cities: Vilna and Frankfurt am Main   115

    A Tale of Two Centers: Israel and the United States   132

Notes   141

Glossary   142

Selected Reading List   148

■

Religious Traditions of the World

One of human history's most fascinating aspects is the richness and variety of its religious traditions—from the earliest times to the present, in every area of the world. The ideal way to learn about all these religions would be to visit the homeland of each—to discuss the scriptures or myths with members of these traditions, explore their shrines and sacred places, view their customs and rituals. Few people have the luxury of leisure and money to take such trips, of course; nor are many prepared to make a systematic study of even those religions that are close at hand. Thus this series of books is a substitute for an around-the-world trip to many different religious traditions: it is an armchair pilgrimage through a number of traditions both distant and different from one another, as well as some situated close to one another in time, space, and religious commitment.

Individual volumes in this series focus on one or more religions, emphasizing the distinctiveness of each tradition while considering it within a comparative context. What links the volumes as a series is a shared concern for religious traditions and a common format for discussing them. Generally, each volume will explore the history of a tradition, interpret it as a unified set of religious beliefs and practices, and give examples of religious careers and typical practices. Individual volumes are self-contained treatments and can be taken up in any sequence. They are introductory, providing interested readers with an overall interpretation of religious traditions without presupposing prior knowledge.

The author of each book combines special knowledge of a religious tradition with considerable experience in teaching and communicating an interpretation of that tradition. This special knowledge includes familiarity with various languages, investigation of religious texts and historical development, and direct contact with the peoples and practices under study. The authors have refined their special knowledge through many years of teaching and writing to frame a general interpretation of the tradition that is responsible to the best-known facts and is readily available to the interested reader.

Let me join with the authors of the series in wishing you an enjoyable and profitable experience in learning about religious traditions of the world.

H. Byron Earhart
Series Editor

Preface

This small volume is an attempt to provide, in a concise and direct way, an introduction to the remarkable religious force and range of Judaism. An effort has therefore been made to present something of the historical diversity and complex variations of Judaism, as well as of its central and dynamic features. Over the course of the centuries, Judaism has never had a fixed or frozen form. Rather, it has expressed itself as a living historical phenomenon in ever new though identifiable variations. Basic beliefs and ideas as well as fundamental texts and rituals have all been subject to interpretation and reinterpretation. The animating forces of creativity, which have shaped the development of Judaism in and through its traditional texts and expressions of observance, are still alive in our own day.

In presenting this book to students and lay readers, it is my pleasure to thank various people. H. Byron Earhart, the series editor, was kind enough to invite me to participate in this educational project on Religious Traditions of the World. I am grateful for his courtesy and promptness in responding to my evolving ideas concerning the arrangement and content of the volume. Various working drafts were tried out in the framework of courses on Judaism taught at Stanford University and at Brandeis University. Among my students, I am particularly grateful to Sebastiano C. Paiewonsky of Brandeis for his close reading of a working manuscript version of the book. His reactions to matters of style and content have been helpful.

As with all my work, I have had the joy to share this book with my wife, Mona. Many thoughts were talked through with her long before they reached the written page; and once my words became a written text, her sharp editorial eye and concrete judgment improved the work in many ways. My gratitude is lifelong.

In completing this work, I have had the special pleasure of the interest and involvement of my oldest son, Eitan. He did research on and provided the initial drafts for the Glossary accompanying this book. I am therefore delighted to acknowledge his assistance both here and in the Glossary itself. My youngest son, Elisha, provided expert help with pagination. I want to thank him very much as well.

Most of the photographs found in the book are courtesy of Bill Aron, who has allowed me to use materials from his collection *From the Four Corners of the Earth* as well as from unpublished material. I am also grateful to the American Jewish Historical Society, located at Brandeis University, for additional photographs and for archival assistance.

■

Chronology of
Jewish Religious History

Dates	Major Cultural and Religious Events
2000 to 1250 B.C.E.*	—ancestors of the Jews migrate from Mesopotamia to the land of Canaan —formation of nomadic and early settlement traditions of the patriarchs; development of tribal lineages
1250 to 1050 B.C.E.	—exodus from Egyptian bondage; formation of covenantal community; conquest and initial settlement of Cannan —development of tribal structures and forms of national leadership
1050 to 587/6 B.C.E.	—rise and establishment of monarchy under David (ca. 1013–973); First Temple built by Solomon, son of David —development of ancient Israelite institutions and literature; religious creativity; emergence of

*B.C.E. indicates Before the Common Era; C.E. indicates the Common Era.

	classical prophecy with Amos (mid-eighth century)
	—Assyrians conquer Samaria; exile of ten northern tribes (722/1 B.C.E.)
	—Jerusalem temple and Judea destroyed by Babylonians; exile of Judeans to Babylon (587/6)
539 B.C.E. to 70 C.E.	—beginning of return to Zion; restoration of ancient institutions and leadership; Temple rebuilt (515) and prophecy revived
	—emergence of classical Judaism, centered around the law (revelation) and its interpretation (traditions)
	—rise of Greek power and hegemony in Palestine (331); Judaism prohibited by Antiochus IV, Maccabees revolt (168), and Temple restored and purified (165)
	—development of different religious groups in Palestine, including the community around the Dead Sea; and the development of Jewish life in Alexandria; Philo combines Jewish culture with Hellenistic thought

—emergence of Pharisees as
dominant religious movement,
and its consolidation of the ideals
of scholarship and piety

—rise of Roman rule; conquest of
Palestine in 63 B.C.E.

70 to 700 C.E. —rabbinic Judaism in formation;
development of class of sages and
rabbinical schools of study and
interpretation

—fall of Second Temple to Romans
(70); Rabbi Yochanan ben
Zakkai founds center for legal
study and administrative rule in
Yavneh (Jamnia); conference on
canonization of biblical literature
at Yavneh (90)

—Rabbi Judah the Prince compiles
the Mishnah, the written digest
of the oral traditions and rules of
the Tannaim

—establishment of Babylonian
rabbinical academies and the
development of vast
commentaries on the Mishnah,
called Talmud, by Amoraim;
consolidations of these comments
and other traditions produce
Palestinian and Babylonian
Talmuds (mid-fifth–sixth
centuries)

—Midrashic (nonlegal) creativity in
Palestine and Babylonia

700 to 1750 C.E.   —consolidation of legal traditions
and liturgy; Massoretes establish
traditional text of the Bible
(Rabbinic Bible)
—Jewish life spreads from Israel to
Spain, Morocco, Iraq, and
beyond; development of Jewish
institutions and literary creativity
—Jewish life influenced by
Christianity and Islamic
civilizations
—repeated persecutions and
massacres of Jews, as in the
Rhineland (1040); York,
England (1190); Navarre
(1328); Spain (1391); Poland;
(1648). Ritual burning of
Talmud in Paris (1244) and Italy
(1553)
—repeated exile of Jews, as from
England (1291), France (1309),
Spain (1492), and Portugal
(1496); ghetto introduced in
Venice in 1516
—major thinkers (most notably
Rashi, in 1040) emerge to
comment upon or consolidate the
biblical and rabbinical traditions;

development of systematic
philosophical expressions of
Jewish theology (most notably by
Maimonides, born in 1128);
emergence of new trends in
Jewish mysticism in Spain and
Germany (*Zohar* is written in
Spain in the late 13th century)
—revival of Jewish mysticism in
Safed, Palestine (sixteenth
century), led by Joseph Karo and
Isaac Luria; major compilation of
Jewish law by Karo (*Shulkhan
Arukh*)
—important period of Talmudic
study in Poland
(sixteenth–eighteenth centuries)
—Jewish community founded in
New Amsterdam, New York in
1654

1750 C.E. to present   —emergence of new patterns of
Jewish life, due to social and
ideological revolutions in Europe
and challenges to old rabbinical
structures in Eastern Europe
—development of secular Jewish
enlightenment and religious
reform movements in Western
Europe; pietistic revival, known
as Hasidism, under spiritual

leadership of Rabbi Israel Baal
Shem, in Eastern Europe;
resistance of traditional
Orthodoxy in Eastern Europe;
accommodations to European
culture develop in the West
—spread of new religious
developments to America in the
nineteenth century; foundation of
Union of American Hebrew
Congregations (Reform) in 1873
and of the Jewish Theological
Seminary of America
(Conservative) in 1886
—revival of Jewish nationalism,
called Zionism, from 1881;
Herzl writes Zionist manifesto
(*The Jewish State,* 1896), and
the Zionist movement is founded
in 1897; resettlement of land of
Israel and revival of Hebrew
language; Tel Aviv founded in
1909
—Nazi war against the Jews of
Europe, 1933–45; six million
Jewish noncombatants murdered
during World War II;
development of Jewish resistance
in Europe (Warsaw Ghetto
uprising, 1943); resistance
spreads to Jews in Palestine

—Jews return en masse to land of
Israel and develop social,
cultural, and political
institutions; state of Israel
founded in 1948
—partition of Palestine between
Jews and Arabs; frequent
conflicts; Six Day War (1967)
and Jewish reunification of
Jerusalem; ancient temple wall
recovered and ancient holy sites
declared accessible to all
—revival of Jewish cultural and
religious institutions in America;
cultural ties deepened between
Jews of Israel and Diaspora

■

CHAPTER I

Introduction

L et us imagine the following historical event, one quite typical of Jewish life as it has been practiced worldwide for over two thousand years. On a **Sabbath*** day sometime in the mid-sixteenth century, the Jews of Cochin, a city on the Malabar coast of southwest India, gather in the **synagogue** for worship. On that day the readings from the Bible include chapters from the book of Exodus and a portion of Chapter 46 from the prophecies of Jeremiah. The first of these readings recalls the slavery of the ancient Israelites in the land of Egypt (thirteenth century B.C.E.); the second announces a divine promise to a different generation (seventh century B.C.E.) that the nation would one day be restored to its ancestral homeland—the land of **Israel**—from all the far-flung lands of its dispersion. Reflecting on these matters, the **rabbi** or learned elder tells those assembled that the history and the hope just read from the Bible are not just words from the past. They are, he says, living words for them: the slavery in Egypt is their own national memory and the promise of national renewal their own collective hope. Hearing this, the congregation nods assent—just as they are doing in a synagogue in Alexandria on that same Sabbath, when Rabbi David **ben** Solomon ibn Abi Zimra gives his learned address, and just as they are doing in a synagogue in Palestine, after the discourse of the mystic and lawyer Rabbi Joseph Karo.

Thus, though separated east and west and ruled by all the kingdoms of the earth, the Jews the world over were and are one people sharing deep bonds despite external differences of custom and costume. They share similar national memories and hopes rooted in the

---

*Terms defined in the Glossary are printed in boldface where they first appear in the text.

11

same biblical texts, which they read yearly and in the same sequence. And they also share a book of common prayers for everyday worship and a fixed pattern of observances for every moment of the calendar year. In this way the teachings and **commandments** of the Bible, as explained or reformulated by scholars throughout the centuries, have been faithfully preserved and lovingly performed by Jews from Cochin to Kracow and from Bombay to Brooklyn—all to the glory and honor of God.

Judaism is thus the religious expression of the Jewish people from antiquity to the present day as it has tried to form and live a life of holiness before God. It is, on the one hand, an expression of recognizable uniformity, practiced commonly and communally by Jews across the centuries in different lands. But, on the other, it is also a religious expression with great historical variations. Never static, Judaism has changed and challenged its adherents for over two millennia, even as it has been changed and challenged by them in different circumstances and times. This relationship of continuity and change stands at the center of Jewish practice and belief. Since Judaism characteristically understands itself by commenting on its own earlier traditions, let us follow this lead and turn, by way of introduction, to two most instructive texts.

The first of these is a remarkable legend preserved in the Babylonian **Talmud**, the foremost collection of classical Jewish law and lore (edited in the fifth century C.E., but containing traditions from up to 750 years earlier). In just a few sentences, the narrative discloses the authoritative core of Jewish creative vigor and the very pulse of its unity within diversity. It shows Judaism to be at once a religion rooted in the Bible—in terms of its beliefs and behaviors, history and hopes—yet radically transformed by the ongoing teachings of the sages. All this is conveyed in a series of dramatic folk images (not abstract arguments) that extend literary hints found in the Bible itself.

The text has its point of departure in the biblical account of the revelation of the divine Law at Mount Sinai as recorded in the book of Exodus. In the Bible, this is the central moment of ancient Israelite history and religion, for it is the moment, according to tradition, when the ancient Hebrews became a religious nation bound to God. Understandably, then, the divine revelation at Sinai has remained the central religious event for Jews and Judaism ever since. But when we look closely at the biblical text, which apparently only states that the Israelites received the Ten Commandments and a rather limtied collection of ordinances at Sinai, we might well wonder how this event, could also be the source of the voluminous laws and practices of historical Judaism.

The biblical passage (in Exodus 19) simply states that, while the nation waited below, "**Moses** ascended" the mountain to receive God's laws and instructions for them. However, according to Rab, the teacher (third century C.E.) in whose name the legend was transmitted in the Talmud[1], this textual reference is merely an allusion to a more profound spiritual moment for Moses and the future Jewish people. It is but the merest clue of what "really" took place on that occasion—namely, Moses' spiritual ascension to heaven. There, the legend tells us, the future lawgiver Moses found God adding little scribal flourishes to the letters of the Law, the **Torah**. Astonished and perplexed, Moses asked for an explanation. God then told him that a man would arise after many generations, **Akiba** ben Joseph by name, who would be able to derive "heaps of laws" from each jot and tittle of the Torah. Moses was thus given to understand that the written Law, which he was to receive from God and transmit to the nation, would be adapted to ever new historical situations through creative interpretations of even the smallest of its letters and calligraphic ornaments.

The legend relates that Moses wished to see this man and was granted his request. Turning around, Moses found himself in an academy of study where Akiba and his disciples were expounding the Torah (over a thousand years later). Thereupon, Moses sat himself in the rear of the hall among the novices and tried to follow the proceedings, but he was thoroughly dumbfounded. At long last, a student asked Akiba the basis for his argument and was told, "It is a law given to Moses at Sinai." Thus the new ruling was assured through having its basis and authority in the ancient written Torah of God. Hearing this, Moses was comforted. But then a deeper perplexity forced him to ask God, "Master of the Universe, you have such a man (as Akiba, who can elaborate the Torah to such an extent) and you give the Torah by me?!" "Be silent," answered God, "for this is how I have determined it."

Formulated in the first centuries of Judaism, this legend is very much a Jewish "myth of origins," for in the manner of myth the

Torah scribe. The task of copying a Torah scroll is one of great piety and rigor. All details have been fixed by tradition. Photo credit: Bill Aron.

account provides a charter of authority for the basic ways and worldview of the culture. In this case, it serves to anchor the numerous and apparently nonbiblical legal expositions of the rabbis—the authoritative teachers of Judaism—in the most formative and primary document of Judaism: the Bible. It recounts for a later Jewish audience, subject to the Torah and its binding interpretations, how God prepared the basis for the oral teachings of the sages when the written Torah was divinely inscribed and given to Moses at Mount Sinai. Indeed, the audience is drawn behind the biblical narrative and into a mythic realm where the vast historical and spiritual unfoldings of Judaism are formally anticipated and justified. In the words of another formulation of this ideology: "Everything which a disciple of the wise (a rabbinic sage) might ever innovate was already given to Moses at Sinai." From the revealed Torah of God at Sinai, say the rabbis, flows a continuous revelation of teachings through their authoritative expositions.

Another dimension of this "myth of origins" pertains to the actions or rituals that accompany the words and give them dramatic expression. A correlation between "sacred words" (Gk., *mythoi*) and "sacred actions" (Gk., *dramata*) is a common feature of primitive and ancient religions. But it is also a feature of the great world religions, and recurs in Judaism in various forms. In the present case, the text depicts a relationship between sacred words (the Torah) and ritual (Torah study) that is historically actualized whenever the written Torah is renewed through study and interpretation. From this perspective, every student of the Law renews through interpretation the first giving of the Torah at Sinai and extends that revelation into new historical circumstances. This, of course, is the mysterious relationship between Torah and interpretation that God communicates to Moses in the legend, for Moses, the lawgiver, needs sages like Akiba for the sake of the ongoing life of the Torah, just as each sage (like Akiba) regards Moses as the first teacher of Judaism, whose Torah is the basis of all authoritative teaching. Without the studious deliberation of an Akiba, Moses' ancient text would become a dead letter. But without the Torah of Moses, the expositions of the sages would lack religious authority. It must therefore come as no surprise that, in time, Moses was called *rabbeynu,* "our rabbi." And so it has remained.

The revelation of divine instructions (the Torah) at Sinai is thus a central historical moment for Judaism and its history: it is the time when God and the ancestors of the Jews entered into a religious relationship, or **covenant**, based on these very teachings. In a strictly historical sense, therefore, the revelation at Sinai was a "once and only" time for Jewish religious destiny. But as we have seen, this event has also been something more than a one-time occurrence for Jews and Judaism: it has been something of a mythic moment, recurring "always and again" whenever the Torah is studied and its teachings interpreted. Thus the divine voice heard at Sinai does not cease, according to the traditional Jewish self-understanding, but is authoritatively developed through the human words of the sages. It is they who faithfully renew the event of Sinai and who generate "heaps of laws" that extend the covenant into new areas of life. In fact, for Judaism, no area of life was or is in principle excluded from this process: every action and behavior, no matter how seemingly mundane, could be transformed into an expression of religious piety. For this reason, Judaism has often been called a positive religion, a religion that prescribes and regulates all the actions of its adherents. Through devoted obedience to the prescriptions of the Torah and its rabbinic elaborations, Judaism has taught that one might lead a life of divinely guided sanctity and ascend along just this path to religious perfection and communion with God.

For Judaism, then, the Torah and its vast tradition of interpretation is an elaborate but sure guide to holy living and nearness to God. But, as we have already suggested, Judaism is also a highly varied religion. It is not only a stable complex of beliefs and behaviors developed over millennia; it is also a religion capable of sustaining ideals and attitudes of the most diverse—and seemingly contradictory—sort. For example, in contrast to the above-mentioned focus on interpretation and formal observance of the commandments, there is a strand in Judaism that allows for a more spontaneous, simple meeting between a person and God. This feature of simple, unmediated encounters with the divine is exemplified in a legend found in the *Book of the Pious* from thirteenth-century Germany—nearly a thousand years after our rabbinic "myth" of Akiba and Moses.[2]

This legend tells of a herdsman who did not know how to pray, though it was his custom every day to say: "Lord of the world! Surely you know that if you had cattle and gave them to me to tend, though I would take wages from all others, from you I would take nothing—because I love you!" And so time passed. But a learned man who was going on his way, came upon the herdsman praying thus, and said to him, "Fool, do not pray in this way." And when the herdsman asked him how to pray, the learned man taught him the traditional order of the prayers and all their set words. Thus it was that the herdsman ceased praying in his customary way. In time, however, the herdsman forgot what he had been taught and stopped praying altogether. He was even afraid to pray in his old style, for the learned man had told him not to. And so it was. But then one night the learned man had a dream and in it a voice said, "If you do not tell him to pray as he did before you came to him, know that evil will befall you, for you have robbed me of one who belongs to the world to come." And this the learned man did. "Behold," concludes the legend, "here there is neither Torah [study] nor works [obedience to the Law], but only this, that there was one who had it in his heart to do good, and he was rewarded for it, as if this were a great thing. For (tradition teaches that) 'the Merciful One desires the heart.' Therefore let people think good thoughts, and let these thoughts be turned to the Holy One, Blessed be He."

It is evident that this legend undercuts the Torah "myth" presented earlier, for here neither learning nor legal piety constitutes a life of holiness with God, only simplicity and purity of heart. Likewise, in this text God is not far off and mediated through the cultural traditions of the religious community, but near to anyone whose soul seeks the divine Presence without guile or self-consciousness. The holy herdsman is thus the opposite of the sage. He is both unsophisticated and natural, equally unaware of the Torah and its vast tradition of learning and practice. For him, religious devotion is not structured by a community of believers who share communal symbols and language; nor can he even effectively receive this communal heritage or make good use of it. Though taught the normative religious practices of Judaism by the sage, the herdsman soon forgets his instructions and becomes nonobservant. Indeed, it is the sage who is reproved by God in this legend, as his wise counsel has deprived heaven of an act of pure service.

For a classical tradition that had repeatedly affirmed the ancient rabbinic dictum that "a simple person cannot be pious" since such a one does not know the Law, the divinely given guide to piety, the legend of the herdsman is a powerful critique of essential values. Indeed, what is portrayed here is a piety that can be neither learned nor transmitted; nor is it divinely taught. The core of authentic religion, the legend counsels, is the authentic heart of the worshipper—his or her selfless humility. And it is just this service that God wants.

Taking both legends in hand, we go a long way toward understanding the powerful tensions and balances that have structured Judaism over the ages. Such tensions and balances have provided mechanisms whereby Judaism could revise or critique itself for the sake of its ongoing integrity. In the first case, we noted the dynamic relationship Judaism posits between the ancient Torah of Sinai and the ongoing interpretation of the sages. In the latter instance, the apparent tension between a "piety of strict obedience" and a "piety of simple spontaneity" has also proved salutary and regenerative for Judaism. Where the one or the other pole has predominated in Jewish history, it was counterbalanced by its opposite. In this way the observance of the divine Law, which could not be abrogated, was dynamically infused with the spirit of spontaneity, and the power of spontaneous worship of God was always structured by the norms of the community. Indeed, a balance was always struck—in each community and by each person—between what was called "the yoke of the commandments" and "the yoke of the kingdom of heaven." Their indissoluble combination is one of the unique and characteristic features of the religion, for it posits that there is no simple love of God that is not concretized through some customary form of behavior and no strict observance of these behaviors that is not also to be regarded as an expression of the love of God. According to one classic statement, the combination of these two values explains why the liturgical affirmation of divine unity and lordship, the **Shema**— "Hear, O Israel, the Lord is our God, the Lord is One"—is immediately followed by the exhortation: "You shall love the Lord, your God, with all your heart, with all your soul, and with all your might; and let these words which I [God] command you this day be upon your heart . . . " Not content with observing that this prayer derives from a sequence of biblical citations (Deut. 6:4 ff.), the ancient rabbis explained the first as an acknowledgment of divine sovereignty and the second as an injunction to practice the Law (the commandments) of God. First one accepts "the kingdom of heaven" (God's majesty), they said, then one assumes "the yoke of the commandments" (the Torah and its interpretation).

On the basis of the two legends discussed above, Judaism may be defined as the religious expression of the Jewish people based upon a Torah believed given them by God and on the teachings of this Torah as elaborated by trained sages for the sake of sanctifying human behavior and guiding nearness to God. To be sure, precisely because Judaism is a historical religion, every element of this definition—God, the Jewish people, Torah, and its interpretation—has undergone significant development or change. To speak, therefore, of Judaism as some timeless essence would be as misleading as asserting that, because of its historical variations, Judaism is a disconnected miscellany of beliefs and behaviors. The fact is that a fairly stable pattern of behaviors and beliefs has marked the expressions of traditional Judaism from classical times (the first centuries of our era) to the present day. Accordingly, if the very *history* of Judaism precludes our speaking of an abstract "essence of Judaism," one can nevertheless speak of its "essential features." This is constituted by the several elements of the definition. To better appreciate this unity (of stable elements) within diversity (of historical expressions), let us now retrieve some of the issues introduced in the preceding pages and say a bit more about them.

The Jews

Judaism is rooted in the people who have constituted it, beginning with the ancient Israelites of biblical times and continuing on down through all those who have assumed its traditions. These people are the Jews, whose name derives from a Hebrew word referring to the citizens of ancient Judea, part of the biblical land of Israel in Greco-Roman times (second century B.C.E.–fifth century C.E.). According to the biblical record, the ancestors of the Jews originated in families and tribal units who wandered from ancient Mesopotamia to the land of Canaan (some time in the mid-second millennium B.C.E.). The Bible presents this movement and settlement as based upon a divine call and promise to an ancestor named Abraham. With this call, a religious bond, or covenant, was established between Abraham and his descendants and his God. From the first, this covenantal bond and its ritual expression (**circumcision** of males) gave the people a self-conscious religious destiny. They were henceforth not solely part of the natural seed of Adam, the mythic progenitor of humankind, but part of the divinely constituted seed of Abraham, the bearers of special promises about settlement in the land of Canaan. Few ritual obligations are described at this early point in the Bible. It is only with the expansion of this covenant to all the multitudinous descendants of Abraham who came out of Egyptian bondage (in the mid-thirteenth century B.C.E.) that a true religious peoplehood was constituted. This came about through the divine covenant with the nation of Israel at Sinai. With it and its obligations, Israel and all of its descendants assumed their special spiritual destiny as "a priestly kingdom and a holy nation" (Exodus 19:6).

The people thus believed themselves doubly chosen: once in the time of Abraham and again in the time of Moses. And yet all persons could join this nation on the condition that they keep the covenant and fulfill its obligations. Thus ancient Israel combined two patterns of affiliation known to religions of antiquity. On the one hand, the nation of Israel was a "natural" people constituted by a special religious life, so that all those born into the nation were Israelites and practitioners of the Mosaic covenant law. This is a type of religious ethnicity well represented by the ancient Greeks and Chinese. In it one is born into a tribal unit or confederation and goes on to practice its customs and ceremonies. But beginning in the Hellenistic world, around the time of the earliest formations of Judaism (from the third century B.C.E.), there also developed the phenomenon sometimes referred to as "religions of salvation." These religions were not at all based on such primary affiliations as birth or descent, but rather on secondary associations assumed through special initiation ceremonies or rites of conversion. The so-called mystery cults of the Greeks and Romans as well as the early and later Christian church represent this type of spiritual affiliation. To be sure, the society of ancient Israel in early biblical times had already developed procedures for the incorporation of non-Israelites into its covenant community with full ethnic and ritual rights (through marriage for women; through circumcision for males). But when Judaism in Hellenistic times also developed an ideology and practice of conversion, propagandizing its theology and truth claims to pagans, this was an altogether new development. It opened Judaism to more spiritual forms of affiliation.

In sum, Judaism combined (and still combines) two modes of religious association. The first derives from ancient Israel and pertains to the ancient ethnic core of the Jewish people. The second mode of affiliation also derives from antiquity, but it took on new forms in the classical period of the religion. Through it Judaism extended its divine covenant to anyone who would believe that the Torah is a divinely revealed way of holiness and salvation and who would practice that "way." Once converted by established procedures, such persons are Jews in all respects and their descendants are fully Jews "by nature" as it were. In the sense that Judaism is both grounded in a closed religious-ethnic community and open to all who would accept its teachings, the religion of Judaism includes both particularistic and universalistic elements. Other aspects of this combination of opposites, such as the fact that Jews have believed themselves divinely chosen via Abraham from among all the descendants of Adam for a particular covenantal destiny that includes a universal mission of witness to their God's teachings and reality, will be mentioned further on.

God

As indicated, the self-understanding of the Jewish people was and is that of a distinct people, a people whose uniqueness is constituted by its spiritual link with God and expressed through the ritual and ethical requirements of the covenant (the Torah and its traditional elaborations). God is therefore central to Judaism, but not in any abstract or impersonal sense. Rather, God is always the One *who* establishes a covenant, *who* reveals the Torah, *who* requires obedience and sanctity, *who* guides the people's destiny, and so on. This is particularly true of Judaism's central monotheistic proclamation (the Shema) that God is One and Unique. Such a creed was always taken to mean that the God who made a covenant with Moses, delivered the people of Israel from slavery in Egypt, revealed the Torah, and made a covenant with the entire nation at Sinai is the one and only God in the universe. To be sure, abstract formulations of the sovereignty or perfection of this God can be found in Jewish philosophical literature, and daring speculation on the hidden life or nature of divinity also recurs in the long history of Jewish mysticism. But even in these two cases of rational arguments and theological insights about God, the centerpoint for the religion remained the historical moment of divine revelation—the event of personal contact between God and the people of Israel at Sinai—and its ongoing covenantal implications. As a result, the active religious life of the Jew is not one of theory and deduction, but one entirely filled with ritual and moral obligations constantly making the reality of God present in the most personal and concrete terms.

This feature of personal divine immediacy marks all the ritual sanctifications of life in Judaism, quite apart from whatever abstract theological system may justify it at more theoretical levels. For example, this immediacy is found in the traditional expressions of thanskgiving for blessings received from God, *who provides* all forms of life and sustenance (as in the standard liturgical formulation: "Blessed are you, O Lord our God, king of the universe, *who brings forth food from the ground"* or *"who clothes the naked,"* etc.); and it is found in diverse expressions of hope for blessings to be received from God, *who may provide* them in the present or future (as in the liturgical phrases: *"May you heal us,* O Lord, that we may be healed.... *May you restore us* to you.... *May you hear our prayer''*).

Reflecting on these two aspects of the religion, we may state that in its more developed forms Judaism is a two-tiered system that balances or integrates abstract concepts of God with notions and experiences of God as a personal covenantal Presence. But, this granted, it is vital to remember that the daily *life* of the religion is predicated on the latter, for Judaism is not just a "monotheism" in any abstract sense, but a "covenantal monotheism" in the specific sense in which it expresses a belief in one God who has chosen Israel from among the nations and revealed to it the Torah—for its obedience, holiness, and redemption. It is just this "covenantal monotheism" that has structured and conditioned the religious imagery and experience of God in Judaism over the ages.

Torah and Interpretation

Jewish covenantal monotheism can furthermore be seen to have a rule-governed, legal character. Everything is strictly regulated by the teachings and commandments of the Torah: eating, personal relations, work, and much more. Indeed, what is not explicitly set forth in the Torah of God is derived from or related to it by the interpretations of the sages over the centuries. There are thus three major intersecting structures of authority in Judaism: God, the Torah, and the interpretation of Torah by qualified sages. In theory, each of these structures is independent, though in actuality they converge and interrelate dynamically. Thus, though it is believed that God expresses his will in the Torah for all time, it is the sages who explicate and apply this will for all historical situations. This, of course, is the essential point of the Talmudic legend about Moses discussed earlier. In another striking expression of this ideology, the sages actually deny any authoritative role to divine intervention in their legal discussions. The reason provided is most striking. "It [the Torah] is not in heaven," states a Talmudic sage (quoting Scripture) when disallowing the substitution of divine miracles for the logic of human interpretation. A final legendary coda reinforces the point: when the whole episode came before God himself, he laughed, we are told, and said, "My sons have defeated Me!"[3]

Tradition

The cumulative result of the converging authority structures of God, Torah, and interpretation is *tradition*—itself an authority structure and religious reality of major significance in Judaism. On the one hand, tradition embodies the cumulative legal and theological teachings of the sages in writings that have themselves assumed an aura of sanctity. But tradition also includes the sum of customary beliefs and practices of Jews at all times, though with specific reference to those features that are culturally alive for Jewish communities at any given period. And as with the rabbinic literary collections, these customs are also dignified by a religious, sacred aura, for they are believed to be generated out of Jewish living rooted in Torah piety. Such customs include what ancient Jewish authors referred to as "the traditions of the ancestors," many of which were eventually justified by linking them to scriptural passages (through interpretation), and all the variety of folkways and regional embellishments of legal practices that have thickened the atmosphere of Jewish life, affecting its styles and gestures, its cuisine and clothing, its language and imagery. Thus if the divine law together with the authoritative teachings of the sages came collectively to be known as "Torah," a medieval maxim even went so far as to add that "the customs of Israel are [also!] Torah." Though few Jews over the centuries would have denied this essential cultural equation because they did indeed experience the totality of Jewish life as "Torah," many objected to so sharp a formulation. In any event, for a Jew born into the lived reality of Jewish practice, tradition is the crown of all crowns, the total life-breath of Judaism.

The massive scope of the Jewish tradition and its fluid extension into every aspect of life constitute for the traditionalist nothing short of the immediate covenantal Presence of God at all times. The ancient theological dictum "there is no place devoid of him (God)" might thus with valid reason be applied to tradition as well, both as regards its pervasive scope and, as suggested above, as regards its functional character as a token of divine reality in the life of the Jew. In the ongoing history of Judaism, in which the prescriptions of the sacred Torah have been safeguarded and extended by many levels of tradition (interpretation and custom), this tradition has itself become sacred. The result is that it, too, has been extended by many new levels of interpretation and authoritative custom. For Jews over the centuries, this complex pattern of life woven around the written Torah has been the sure way to God because it was the traditional way. Some even went so far as to believe that the entirety of traditional belief and practice was an expression of the will of God—an absolute value in its own right—though other Jews felt that something like the critique of the "holy herdsman" was necessary to caution the faithful that the garment of tradition was a means to holiness—not an end in itself.

In the preceding pages, we have taken some initial steps toward an understanding of Judaism. Through an introduction to its essential matrix of elements, Judaism was presented as a covenantal monotheism structured by such core features as God, Israel (the people), Torah, and interpretation. As suggested, these features have functioned organically and dynamically throughout the history of this religion, stabilizing its vast life system and generating new and renewing expressions. Thus, while these essential features have their own distinct histories over the long life of Judaism, their meanings have been further shaped through various recombinations. This has resulted in new hierarchies or orderings of meaning among the features and new modes of interaction among them. The way that God is understood and related to Torah, for example, or how Torah is conceived and related to interpretation and the people of Israel are thus matters of great diversity in the history of Judaism.

Such modifications and resynthesis of essential teachings have served to regenerate the phenomenon of Judaism for over twenty-five hundred years. Indeed, amid a highly inflexible sense of destiny and direction, this remarkable capacity for variation and reemphasis has helped the religion to adapt to new historical features and to transform them into authentic expressions of Jewish life and belief. It is to the historical unfolding of such expressions that we now turn.

CHAPTER II

Judaism as an Ideological System

W hen we think about a religion, many things come to
mind: first, a vast array of ideas, values, and beliefs;
and second, alongside these, a host of verbal and nonverbal features
connected with authoritative persons, symbols, and rituals. Altogether, these many elements combine to express a worldview. Sometimes, in response to a specific question or set of circumstances, only
one or another aspect of the worldview is involved or given direct
expression. More commonly, however, the various beliefs and symbols of a worldview mix with related rituals and values to constitute
a thick cultural web. Indeed, when a religion truly does its cultural
work, its worldview is always being enacted at personal and interpersonal levels. This is as much the case for lay people, who are often
incapable of articulating values and beliefs, as it is for the official
teachers of a given religion.

In line with these considerations, we shall in this chapter treat
Judaism as an ideological system, that is, both as a system of ideas
about God, the world, and persons and as a system of values direct-
ing action and feeling within society. These ideas and values have
not remained fixed throughout Jewish religious history, so it will be
important to pay attention to their *historical* growth and development. Moreover, the ideas and values of historical Judaism have not
always coalesced in just one cultural configuration, so it will also be
important to pay attention to the *varieties of Judaism* that have
come to historical expression. Sometimes one or another of the features of the matrix dominates; and all the while different understandings of the role and meaning of Torah, interpretation, Israel,

and tradition come to expression. Finally, having surveyed Judaism from an ideological and historical perspective, we shall turn our attention to the ritual expression of Jewish belief and value in Chapter III.

Rabbinic Patterns of This-Worldly Holiness and Salvation

The Biblical Heritage

The history of Judaism begins with the Bible and its religious-literary heritage, for the twenty-four books of the Hebrew Bible not only constitute the literary anthology of the religion and culture of ancient Israel, but for Jews and Judaism they comprise *the foundation document* of the religion—*the* text Jews believe to contain the revealed teachings of God given to the house of Israel in antiquity and faithfully studied ever since. The Bible is not, therefore, an "Old Testament" whose historical recollections and religious teachings have subsequently lost their value or authority (wholly or in part). It rather remains *the* book of authoritative teachings and memories for Judaism, *the* work whose proper interpretation constitutes the vitality and authority of ongoing Jewish life.

When we refer to the Bible as the foundation document of Judaism, therefore, at least two important issues must be considered. The first issue is a historical one and is rooted in the fact that Judaism has always perceived its origins to be found *in* the Bible. This perception has several interrelated aspects. First, Jews have viewed the persons in biblical antiquity as their own forebears and the events of that age as their own prehistory. Second, Jews have always considered the covenant between God and the ancient Israelites to be the basis of their own religious obligations. And finally, it has been believed since antiquity that no break whatever separates the religion of the ancient Hebrews and the religion of Judaism, and that the earliest "institutions" of classical Judaism were actually established by Ezra, a priest and scribe whose work is recorded in late biblical books.

The second issue bearing on the Bible as a foundation document is an ideological one and is rooted in the fact that this text has always been regarded as the prime source *of* Judaism. This consideration also has several interrelated aspects. First, Jews have regarded the beliefs and commandments recorded in the Bible as continuous with and continued by Judaism, albeit in highly reinterpreted ways. Second, Jews have always considered the prescriptions and institutions of this text as the model for their own behaviors, again often in radically transformed ways. And finally, it has been a tenet of rabbinic Judaism since antiquity that all the features of Judaism, no matter how innovative, have their ultimate source in the Bible. Indeed, it has been one of the principle tasks of traditional Jewish interpretation to establish just this point and to give it authority.

Now, since Judaism is so profoundly rooted in the Bible, it behooves us to ask what Judaism inherited from ancient Israel by way of the Bible. In purely literary terms, it inherited a vast anthology of texts spanning nearly a millennium or more, from the nomadic traditions of the patriarchs (c. 1500–1350 B.C.E.) to the historical traditions of the Jewish resistance to Hellenism recorded in the book of Daniel (mid-second century B.C.E.). These texts include epic traditions of the Exodus from Egyptian bondage and the conquest and settlement of ancient Canaan, records of the royal courts and sacred shrines, moral teachings and admonitions of the prophets, liturgies and prayers of the kings and commoners, practical advice and speculative wisdom, religious rituals and civil rules, and much more. While certain perspectives dominate, there is no one religious or ideological viewpoint in this large literature. In fact, many viewpoints (prophetic, priestly, monarchic) and many concerns (theological, historical, ethical) are to be found. One thinks, for example, of the diverse religious expressions of the northern (Ephraimite) and southern (Judahite) tribes; of the different prescriptions for various observances of the Priestly and Deuteronomic writers (the books of Leviticus and Deuteronomy, respectively); and of the different views of God and the people held by early and late prophets, or even by contemporaries like Jeremiah and Ezekiel. There were thus many "Israels" within the house of ancient Israel in its homeland, just as many Judaisms also constituted the house of Israel in all the lands of its dispersion.

Turning to the content of the Hebrew Bible, one might well wonder what kind of impact a document spanning one thousand years and many perspectives could have on Judaism. But the fact is that several ideological constants can be isolated from the material. These are somewhat evident in the thematic emphases that recur throughout the diverse periods and genres of the Bible. And they had a decisive impact upon the very formation of Judaism, guiding its ongoing appreciation of biblical personalities and events and helping to produce its religious ideology and hierarchy of values as well.

The Bible begins at the beginning, with an account of the creation of a habitable world by an almighty and sovereign God. Constrained by neither other gods nor nature, this God forms a good and bounteous world and gives over its stewardship to human care. Thus from the outset, being the product of a good and caring God, the world is presented as compatible with human creativity and salvation. One need not reject the natural world to experience divine grace, for, indeed, such grace is found in the creation itself—in the physical environment (called "good") and in persons (called "very good"). It is only through human disobedience to the directives of this God that pain, death, and lack enter the world. Thus humans, created in the divine image, are free to obey or disobey this Lord—but they and their descendants will bear the consequences of their actions. God is therefore portrayed as a moral judge who is attentive to human action and who responds to it.

These several elements assume new forms as the biblical focus shifts from humans in general to a group chosen from among all peoples and tongues—the Hebrews, the ancestors of the Jews. The process begins with the responsiveness of the great ancestors of this people (Abraham, Isaac, and Jacob) to the demands of this God and their faithfulness to his promises of national blessing in a special homeland—the land of Canaan, later called the land of Israel. This divine promise of national blessing within history is the ancestral covenant, renewed and expanded centuries later for the entire nation. At Sinai, after their divine redemption from Egyptian bondage, the people willingly responded to the obligations and promises revealed by God: they acknowledged his ongoing care and averred faithfulness to him alone.

The stipulations of the covenant, preserved in the Torah, thus constitute the legal-religious bond between the people and their God. Through obedience to the commandments, the nation would find peace and rest in its homeland under a just king. But disobedience to the commandments, the fruit of sin, would result in natural peril and blight, national exile and the whirlwind of flight. Thus, again, it was believed that God was personally attentive to all the details of Israel's life and would judge them accordingly. As the divine covenant was deemed comprehensive, providing a collection of instructions embracing all the details of life (moral, civil, and religious), so was it also believed to be comprehensible, providing a framework of meaning that allowed the people to know and perform God's will. From the perspective of the covenant, moreover, no matter was believed too insignificant for God's concern. Accordingly, history was no meaningless barrage of events and nature was no blind force. Rather, both were subject to the rule and judgment of God. From the perspective of biblical religious ideology, in fact, the rise and fall of nations and the weal and woe of nature were considered to be God's responses to Israel's covenantal behavior. Not even the arguments of Job would ultimately unsettle this view of the world and human destiny.

In the Bible, then, the context of human action is this world, and it is just here that salvation might be experienced—peace and bounty for the nation and food and family for the individual. The commandments therefore serve both to regulate social and religious behavior and to regulate history and nature, all under God's ultimate rule. As a result, no political or natural state was final. The human world was always renewable through repentant and obedient behavior; but it was also subject to doom and despair through selfishness and sin. Knowing what was to be done and the consequences gives ancient Israelite religion its public, or exoteric, aspect. There were no divine secrets of any human significance that were withheld from the human world, just as there was no secret knowledge to be gained through mysterious means for the sake of salvation. What was needed for piety and salvation was given by God to all: "the hidden things are God's, but the revealed things are ours and our children's forever," reports Moses in the Torah (Deut. 29:28). The instructions are "not in heaven," he adds, but "in your mouth and heart" on earth (Deut. 30:14).

The people of ancient Israel are therefore bidden to serve God with faithfulness and love—in the heart and the home, in the community and the shrine, in the homeland and in exile. This service is, moreover, both a task of holiness for the individual in community and a work of witness for the world at large, for if, in the times of sin and disobedience, the national of Israel would be punished by God through nature and the nations of the world, in the times of repentance and obedience Israel would, correspondingly, be the center of grace and hope toward which all nations would turn. The hope of history was thus the eventual restoration and unification of all the nations of the earth through their acceptance of the teachings of a just and righteous God. This would be the time of universal reconciliation when, in the words of the prophets, the harvest would overlap the time of planting, when swords would be turned into plowshares, and when both Israelite and Gentile would, together, go up to the Temple of the Lord for instruction and for celebration. However painful the longing, this biblical hope was faithfully transmitted from one generation to the next and awaited in this world.

Taken altogether, the Hebrew Bible is thus a national book of memories and hopes, of explanations and instructions, of commandments and covenants, of faithfulness and rebellion, and of benefits and dooms. As events of history, the great acts of divine deliverance recorded therein (like the Exodus) were one-time events. But as events of memory these decisive moments also served as images of hope in times of crisis (like the Babylonian exile). And so the first Exodus was taken over by the prophets as the token of future restorations from servitude, just as the first land settlement typified future returns of members of the nation to their ancestral homeland. In similar ways, the old instructions to Moses were not only revelations of the past, but also rules constantly revised for new times and situations. Collectively, these biblical traditions served the people from generation to generation, providing them with self-definition and historical consciousness as well as with rules governing divine-human and interpersonal relations. As these multiple traditions accumulated, they spun a web around the nation and its imagination. No action or hope, no rule or celebration was conceivable apart from them. The inevitable result, taken in subsequent centuries, was the authoritative formulation of these traditions in one fixed corpus: the Bible. Thereafter, in the words of a medieval adage, "Israel and the Torah [were] one."

The Emergence of Classical Judaism (from the end of the Babylonian exile, 539/8 B.C.E., to the fall of the Second Temple, 70 C.E.)

The traditions and institutions of ancient Israel took on new shapes after the events of 587/6 B.C.E., when Jerusalem and Judea were destroyed by Nebuchadnezzar, king of Babylon. At that time, the majority of the Israelites were exiled—with the result that three major geographical centers came to dominate Jewish life and creativity: the province of Judea, in the land of Israel; the region around Alexandria, in the Egyptian delta; and the areas around Babylon, in what is now Iraq. It was, in part, the mixture of these three communities in the land of Israel *after* the return from exile—each with its Torah traditions and practices—that contributed to the controversies of the restoration period. This return to the homeland began in 538 B.C.E. after a decree by Cyrus, the great king of Persia who had just conquered Babylon. Nevertheless, many former Judeans remained in their new homes with their new traditions. In fact, it was the ongoing vitality of these three cultural regions that affected the shapes of Jewish religious expression over the next thousand years.

During the first centuries of national restoration, especially from the time of Alexander the Great (333 B.C.E.) to the early second century C.E., the land of Israel and Alexandria were the dominant religious and cultural centers. Subsequently, the community in Israel remained a recognized center; but, suffering from Roman hegemony, the Jewish institutions of learning and administration in this region were gradually eclipsed by those that had developed in Babylonia. This shift eastward is of considerable historical significance not only because of the emergence of a new geographic sphere of importance (for it was, in many ways, the revival of the old exilic community), but because it also marks a series of decisive shifts in Jewish religious expression, as we shall see.

When the Jews returned to Jerusalem from the Babylonian exile (after 538 B.C.E.), they prepared to rebuild the ancient Temple destroyed a half-century earlier. Soon their ritual practices were restored, and Ezra, the leader of the period, set about to develop a full religious life based on the ancestral Torah of Moses. During this time, the Jews benefited from the benign foreign policy of the Persians. As regional overlords, the Persians actually sought to encourage the revival of native traditions among their vassal populations. Nevertheless, it was inevitable that Persian influences penetrated Jewish life from this early period. A number of religious ideas from ancient Zoroastrianism gradually made an impact and challenged existing beliefs. The Zoroastrian dualistic theology of two supreme gods—one good, the other evil—was naturally rejected by Jews;

but more modified forms of this and other beliefs were gradually absorbed into the stream of developing Judaism. For example, many scholars view the new emphasis on eschatology (theories of the final days) and angelology (role of angels) in Judaism at this time as due to such Persian influence. The literature of the sectarian communities at Qumran (second–first centuries B.C.E.), commonly known as the Dead Sea Scrolls, clearly shows such Eastern influence. In these texts very strong emphasis is given to a separation and rivalry between the cosmic principles of good/light and evil/darkness (though under the rule of one supreme God); to a final cosmic-historical battle in which good/light and purity would be victorious; and to angelology, astrology, notions of personal fate, and so on. Nevertheless, these various ideas and beliefs were skillfully integrated into a viable religious pattern that actually claimed to be the most authentic Jewish expression of the time, one that would be vindicated by God in the end of days.

Unfortunately, very little is really known about this formative period in the history of Judaism—overall. But when Jewish literary sources do fully emerge in the late second century B.C.E., they clearly indicate the vitality of the times. For one thing, the Jews in Egypt, Israel, and Syria were under diverse Greek administrations (the Ptolomies in the south, the Seleucids in the north). This had a great impact on early economic patterns and also on the legal-social forms that entered classical Judaism. In addition, Jews and Judaism fell under the powerful cultural influence of Hellenism. This latter had an inestimable impact, shaping notions of wisdom and Torah study and affecting the language and ideology of Judaism for ages to come. For many Jews in the parochial highlands of Judea, the broad sweep of Hellenism presented unexpected cultural options and ideas. New challenges were in the air, eliciting diverse responses to the competing realities of Greek *paideia* (education and culture) and Torah piety. Three broad types of response can be isolated. Intriguingly, they also foreshadow the dominant patterns of Jewish cultural response to foreign cultures and religions over the centuries. They are *assimilating* into Judaism the foreign ideas and elements, *rejecting* them outright, or *renewing* the religion from within in response to them.

The cosmopolitan and metaphysical scope of Greek speculative thinking and the sophisticated Greek views of intellectual and ethical development made many Jews feel that their native Torah instructions were comparably naive, parochial, and unedifying. As a result, many sought actively to assimilate to the Greek culture, so that they might more fully participate in its alluring intellectual life. Others, just as impressed by the Greek world, nevertheless defended native Jewish traditions and promoted a cultural symbiosis of one sort or another.

Among those who sought a positive response to Hellenism through intellectual creativity, Philo of Alexandria (20 B.C.E.–50 C.E.) must be considered the most significant. As a Jew he was fully devoted to the ancient Torah, an observer of its commandments, and a student of its rabbinical reformulations; but he was just as fully committed to contemporary Greek thought and ideals. Refusing to give up the first for the second, he regarded the instructions of the Torah as of preeminent value and truth. On other hand, he just adamantly refused to reject the path of philosophy as of merely subordinate significance or of no worth. His solution was to adjust the received philosophical tradition (Plato, Aristotle, and the Stoics) to the received Torah tradition (the teachings of Moses and the rabbis) through a sophisticated allegorical procedure. By this means, the divine truths of the Torah were presented not solely as equivalent with philosophical wisdom, but as containing them. Thus no Jew had to reject Torah in order to accept philosophy, for all the truths of philosophy were in the Torah in a most superior manner—if one only knew how to disclose them. Through Philo's guidance, the patriarchal narratives and legislative prescriptions were allegorically revealed to be teachings instructing the philosophical adept in the acquisition and development of spiritual, moral, and intellectual virtues. For example, biblical laws that instructed someone who committed accidental manslaughter to flee to a city of refuge were now shown to be also (in their "deep sense," or Gk. *hyponoia)* concerned with the flight of the human soul from material emcumbrances to God. Similarly, Abraham and Sarah represented not only historical personalities but (again, more deeply) intellectual-moral virtues. In all this, Philo emerges as the first religious philosopher of the West, the first major thinker to integrate philosophical wisdom with divine revelation. In the alien and alluring environment of Alexandria (and elsewhere), Jews could be proud of the philosophical profundity of their ancient heritage (the Torah) and remain observant in practice.

The sophisticated intellectual syncretism of Philo is balanced by the comparably crass religious-intellectual syncretism promoted by some members of the priestly class and aristocracy in Jerusalem. These Jews, through bribery and intrigue, sought to introduce changes in the civil and religious life of Judaism and conspired with the Seleucid overlords to issue decrees the intent of which was to compromise traditional life and observance. In the most significant instance, the Seleucid ruler Antiochus Epiphanes IV was induced to descrate the high altar in the Temple in Jerusalem and require Jews to defile themselves through prohibited acts. What these priests and their followers wanted was nothing short of a hellenization of Judaism. This would have turned the ancestral religion into just one more quasi-philosophical cult in the Hellenistic world. To be sure, their motivations were not entirely narrow-minded or only self-serving. But a majority of Jews soon preceived in these developments a serious challenge to the fundamentals of their national and religious integrity—and they responded accordingly.

Focus on the integrity of the ancestral religion and a violent rejection of foreign influence was thus a second typical response to Hellenism. Of enduring fame in Jewish historical and folk memory are the attacks launched against the Seleucids by a priestly family. Led by one Mattathias and his son, Judah Maccabee, and soon supported by the populace at large, this group won a decisive victory. Reclaiming their heritage from the assimilationists, they were able to repurify and rededicate the sacred Temple in Jerusalem on the 25th of Kislev (November–December), 165 B.C.E.—the day memorialized in the Jewish calendar as Hanukkah and celebrated as the (eight-day) Feast of Dedication. In their deeds and motivations, the Maccabees and their followers reflect the spirit of religious purism and fanatical devotion to native religious tradition that burned deeply in Judaism from the days of the ancient prophets.

The third major type of Jewish expression in this period was one that attempted to effect a dynamic renewal of the religion from within *in response to* outside influences. Rather than accommodating native traditions to new forms or merely rejecting them outright, the Pharisaic way (so-called after the Pharisees, an important rabbinic and lay religious group at this time) was to accommodate the non-native features to the traditions of Torah, to naturalize them, as it were.

Of distinctive significance in early Pharisaism is the emergence of a Torah-centered piety rooted in tradition and interpretation and characterized by a democratic openness to the people as a whole. In fact, the earliest legends and historical fragments about Pharisaic teachers show the emergence of a new type of religious leader: a "disciple of the wise," who was neither priest nor holy man but, characteristically, a self-sustaining lay person who achieved prominence through mastery of the written Torah and the ancient oral traditions. Accordingly, study of the Torah and simplicity of manner remained high ideals of these "disciples," who constituted a fellowship of learning open to all who would study its traditions and practice them. Initially, the ancient oral traditions were not solely authorized by being linked to scriptural passages, but constituted authoritative ancestral lore in and of themselves. By degrees, however, this linkage to Torah was achieved, so that by the end of the first century C.E. Pharisaism was distinguished by its belief that its oral tradition of interpretation was the true elucidation of written Scripture and that it had its origin (in principle, at least) within it.

Torah thus emerged as the absolute center of Pharisaism. All was believed to be contained in it—both the written Torah of Moses and the oral traditions of the "wise"—and the unfolding of the new applications of Torah was considered to be the ongoing historical unfolding of God's infinite word. Accordingly, in Pharisaic Judaism (and this is the pattern of Judaism that has survived to this day) study is a mode of piety. This ideal is noticeable from the earliest records of its founding teachers, like **Hillel**, and has served as the means of cultural-religious renewal ever since. This is not to say that the Greco-Roman environment made no impact on early Pharisaism—it did. But these influences, such as they were, were thoroughly transformed and drawn into the very lifeblood of Judaism. Thus anyone unaware of Stoic ideals of wisdom and sagelike behavior would hardly recognize the impact of these Greek traits upon the popular Pharisaic treatise *Sayings of the Fathers*, just as anyone unaware of Greco-Roman rhetoric and terminology would not perceive their impact upon the methods and terms of classical rabbinic Bible interpretation, so thoroughly naturalized are they. By the same token, Greco-Roman legal patterns and terms were also incorporated into the earliest legal activity of the Pharisaic sages. A celebrated example comes from Hillel. Faced with the refusal of some people to lend money near the Sabbatical Year (every seventh year, during which creditors were required to release debtors from their loans [Deut. 15:1–2]), this sage ingeniously worked out a solution so that the Temple would function as a kind of intermediary between borrowers and lenders. In this way the biblical rule was retained and economic stability restored. Hillel's decree (based on Scripture but going beyond it) was called a *prozbul* in rabbinic law. The term itself is derived from the Greek expression *pros boule*, "before the assembly"; and the very method Hillel used to establish his point was also Greek in origin.[4]

Thus Pharisaism did not attempt to align its teachings either to an alien wisdom or to an alien cultural system but rather sought to integrate the latter into Judaism. In all their work, the Pharisees evince an unswerving conviction in their cultural autonomy and its values; and throughout they project a profound confidence in the truth of the laws and teachings of Scripture. In this, as in other respects, they emerge as the true shapers of historical Judaism.

Rabbinic Judaism in Formation (from the fall of the Temple, 70 C.E., to the redaction of the two Talmuds, fifth-sixth centuries C.E.)

Reflecting on his Jewish heritage and its importance, an early Jewish sage named Simon the Righteous said: "The world depends upon three things: upon Torah, upon Worship (*avodah*), and upon Acts of Loving-kindness."[5] By this he was certainly referring, first, to the centrality in Judaism of Torah and the faithful performance of its commandments; second, to the maintenance of the Temple service (*avodah*) and the proper performance of its rituals; and, third, to a concern for human welfare and the extralegal concern for righteous behavior. Surely all "three things" derive from biblical antiquity: the traditions of the Torah, the celebrations of the Temple, and deeds of social kindness. And surely, too, each of these "three things" was basic in the beneficial maintenance of the divine-human relationship, for the fulfillment of the covenant depended upon obedience to the instructions of the Torah, on the performance of purifications by the priests, and on the expressions of grace and goodwill by all. But when Simon epitomizes these things in just this way he is also giving special power to each for maintaining the flow of divine blessing (natural and historical) to earth. Jews, so to speak, maintain the civilized and beneficent order of life through their actions, for without the teachings of Torah, without the divine-human reconciliations and influences of the Temple, and without gratuitous humanity there would be no "world" whatever—no moral-social order. The institutions of Judaism thus functioned, to speak the language of the sociology of religion, as a system of cultural-cosmic maintenance.

REPLACING THE TEMPLE

The destruction of the Temple in Jerusalem in 70 C.E. and the subsequent desacralization of the Temple Mount by the Romans were thus a major watershed in the history of Judaism. Like all other religions of antiquity, Judaism also gave enormous centrality to its sacral institutions: to the Temple and its priesthood; to the ancient sacrifices of atonement, purification, and thanksgiving; and to the symbolic role of the Temple as the abode of God to which penitents and pilgrims came during seasonal celebrations and times of need. In a word, the Temple established a concrete domain of access to the holy and to divinity; and the priesthood, which controlled the rituals of the Temple, also established or administered the rules of holiness as they pertained to many other spheres of life (like rules of contagion and purification, or rules of required or votary donations). To envisage the loss of the Temple, therefore, would be to envisage religious life without its sacral forms of divine-human intercession, without the possibility of priestly purification for sins and disease, and without the ancient process for divine-human reconciliation.

But ancient Judaism had survived the Babylonian exile without its priestly institutions; and the loss of the Temple in 70 C.E. continued the processes begun centuries before and introduced new transformations. Thus earlier, without their rites and sacrifices, the Babylonian exiles of 587/6 B.C.E. developed new modes of piety (like communal prayer) and generated new treatments of the ancient Torah traditions (particularly their collation, study, and interpretation). During the successive centuries, traces of the increased development of such institutions as synagogues for prayer and houses of study for

the learning and reinterpretation of the Torah can be observed—
alongside, of course, the renewed and still dominant priestly institutions. Accordingly, when the Temple was destroyed, a multifaceted
mechanism was already in place for the survival of a Judaism without sacrifices and the hierarchical authority of the priesthood.

And so two "Houses," the House of Prayer (*beit tefillah*) and the
House of Study (*beit midrash*) replaced the Temple—the House
(*bayit*) par excellence. Each contributed a new understanding of
avodah, or divine service.

THE HOUSE OF PRAYER

In the House of Prayer the language of supplication and praise came
into its own as a distinct form. Prayer was in fact called a "service
(*avodah*) of the heart," whose very order was modeled on the times
of the old Temple sacrifices. We shall consider something of the
forms and content of Jewish Prayer in the next chapter. Here it is
simply necessary to observe, first, that the rabbinic prayer service
was performed thrice daily, morning, afternoon, and evening, like
the sacrifices of old. In addition, this prayer service was also saturat-
ed with recollections of the ancient glory of the Temple and hopes
for its speedy restoration, with reuses of Priestly recitations like the
Priestly benediction (Num. 6:24–26) in the prayer ritual; and with
continued respect for clerical pedigree when honoring individuals to
bless the Torah when it is recited in the communal service. Gradually, recommended and fixed features of the prayer service emerged,
and these were offered to God with all the hopes that such "offerings of the lips" would "find favor" with God, like the sacrifices of
old. "May my prayer be established as fragrant incense before You,"
says the Psalmist (Ps. 141:2). Or in the words of the ancient rabbis,
who only had words to offer: "Be favorable, O Lord our God, towards Your people Israel and their prayer. Restore the Service (*avodah*) to the Shrine of Your House (*bayit*), and lovingly accept the
prayer of Israel. May the service (*avodah*) of Your people be always
favorable before You."[6]

THE HOUSE OF STUDY

This God of Israel, believed to be transcendent above the heavens,
was also believed to be present to the needs of the people. Indeed, as

a majestic and distant Lord, he was called Heaven and King and Power; and as a near and caring Father he was also called Place and Presence and Blessed Holy One. He was referred to as a "seeing eye" and "hearing ear"—an attentive and responsive *personal* God. He was addressed as a God of justice and mercy who, in one striking image, wore phylacteries (prayer boxes, called **tefillin**, with Torah passages inside) just like his earthly servants. In another famous image, this God was portrayed as studying Torah and reviewing the daily interpretations given to it by his people. Thus dignified, the human study of the Torah was also regarded as a major form of religious *avodah*. In fact, the study of the rules of sacrifices found in the Torah was frequently considered to be the post-Temple equivalent of the sacrifices themselves; through the study of the rules for sacrifices it was "as if" they had actually been offered. With the emergence of the House of Study to independent status, Torah replaced Temple; study substituted for sacrifices.

With the removal of sacrifices and priests from the stage of Jewish history, the "disciples of the wise" and their texts moved in to fill the breach. It is therefore hardly fortuitous that, shortly after 70 C.E., the sacred Torah literature was effectively fixed and closed (i.e., canonized). A new stage was thus set for the rabbinic transformation of Scripture. One of the great sages of this period was Rabbi Yochanan ben Zakkai. A figure of history whose deeds were quickly shrouded in legend, Rabbi Yochanan used his political influence with the Roman leadership to have an accredited Pharisaic academy established in the coastal town of Yavneh (also known as Jamnia). Here, in the "vineyard of Yavneh," disciples gathered to revive Judaism from its spiritual and national catastrophe. Much in the manner that contemporary Greeks gathered around their philosophical mentors, Jewish students gathered around their masters and attended to their every deed and word, for all life was the potential sphere of Torah. Thus how the rabbinic master inferred or deduced a legal ruling in this or that circumstance (real or theoretical) or how he comported himself on this or that occasion was of great practical religious importance. A celebrated ideal for a master of this class was "to raise up many disciples," as a contemporary exhortation put it; and for the student the corresponding ideal was "to serve the master gratuitously." As the potential sphere of Torah had "no measure," said the sages, so its spiritual rewards were correspondingly without measure. Torah thus became the consuming ideal of these sages and their students. And with this ideal they helped set Judaism on its new historical course: the academy was the new Temple; the sages were the new priesthood; and the great ritual was the study of Torah.

The vast project of the rabbis, of commenting on the Torah and adapting its teachings to all areas of life, was predicated upon their belief that God's Torah is a "foundation of the world" and that it alone provides a way of truth and holiness on earth. To study the Torah is thus inseparable from its practice, for one can only do God's will if one knows it. Indeed, no two matters than these— knowing the divine will ("study," *talmud torah*) and its performance ("action," *ma'aseh*)—were of greater importance to Judaism. It therefore makes sense to pause here and briefly spell out this project and its major contents.

After 70 C.E., the Torah teachings and rulings of the rabbinical schools (called "houses") of Hillel and Shammai were gathered together, along with other testimonies and interpretations still in oral form. As noted, new academies were set up, first in Yavneh and later in such places in Israel as Usha and Tiberias. In these settings, new rulings were derived from the old Torah, other rules were framed to fill in gaps left by biblical legislation, and a host of theological and homiletical comments were generated from biblical texts to clarify or reinforce Jewish values and perspectives. The gradual result of this "oral Torah"—legal and nonlegal—was the production of a postbiblical rabbinic literature, which was itself then later subject to reinterpretation and elaboration.

The process of textual interpretation is called **midrash**, and the interpretations of Torah for the sake of generating new rules (**halakha**) or justifying (by Scripture) customary ones is known as *midrash halakha*. Such interpretation is part of the native Jewish tradition; its earliest forms are in the Bible itself. It has continued to be the characteristic form of Jewish legal expression over the centuries. This point must be emphasized, for while *midrash halakha* has strong traces in the earliest strata of Jewish literature, the dominant legal work of this time, called the **Mishnah**, is without this explicit exegetical dimension. For this reason, a good deal of the *midrash halakha* that followed it was principally geared to provide (or make explicit) the scriptural basis for the abstractly formulated religious rules recorded in the *Mishnah*.

THE *MISHNAH* AND SUPPLEMENTS

The *Mishnah* is the classical collection of laws and normative rules of behavior of ancient Judaism. In its content, this document reflects the growth and consolidation of halakhic traditions from the preceding centuries and builds upon the earlier (but no longer extant) collections of Rabbi Meier and Rabbi Akiba. The final form of the work is the great religious-intellectual achievement of Rabbi Judah the Prince (the Patriarch of the land of Israel, a political-legal title confirmed by the Romans) sometime in the late second or early third century C.E. It is therefore commonly referred to as "Rabbi's *Mishnah*."

As the written digest of the hitherto exclusively oral traditions of the Tannaim (the Pharisaic sages c. 200 B.C.E.–200 C.E.), the *Mishnah* reflects their legal-religious interests and the majority and minority opinions of their law schools. The abstract formulations and topical structure of the *Mishnah* resembles contemporary Roman codes, and in its content projects the code of behavior Rabbi Judah and the sages sought to impose on the people at large. In the course of time, the *Mishnah* did achieve this grand goal and became and still is *the* foundation document of rabbinic legalism. Subsequent to the Bible, the *Mishnah*, written by the sages, is thus *the* document of Pharisaism emergent and triumphant: the law code of a pattern of Judaism developed by rabbis for themselves and their followers. It soon attained the status of a sacred text.

In terms of its format, the *Mishnah* is divided into six major orders or divisions. These are called Seeds, Feasts, Women, Damages, Holy Matters, and Purities. In turn, each of these orders is subdivided into tractates (totaling sixty-three), and these are then subdivided into smaller teachings called *mishnahs*. The content of the six orders is thus quite complex—more, in fact, than appears at first sight. For example, the order called Seeds comprises rulings on various agricultural issues (like tithing or crop mixtures) but also deals with rules for prayer and gleanings to be left for the poor. The order called Feasts covers rulings dealing with the major holy days (like the Sabbath and **Passover**), but also includes discussions of monetary donations and aspects of the writing of sacred scrolls. The order called Women deals primarily with family laws (like marriage and divorce), but it also includes rules about vows of various sorts. The fourth order, called Damages, covers civil and criminal laws and punishments in all their variety but also deals with matters concerning oaths and idolatry as well as a collection of moral maxims (*The Sayings of the Fathers*). The next order, called Holy Matters, includes sundry ritual rules (like sacrificial offerings, types of sacrilege, and Temple measurements). And the sixth and final order, called Purities, considers impurities attached to such physical states as death, leprosy, or menstruation as well as with their methods of religious purification (through sacrifices or immersion in water).

The above listing does not encompass the entirety of Tannaitic legal material. To it must be added a large "Supplement" to the *Mishnah* with many significant variations (called *Tosephta*), a great many Tannaitic teachings (called *beraitot*) preserved in the Talmud (see presently), and a variety of *ad hoc* decrees and rulings (called *taqqanot* and *gezerot*) issued for the public good. Altogether, this literature (particularly the *Mishnah*) constitutes *the agenda* of rabbinic legal study (both theoretical and practical) over the centuries.

THE TALMUDS

As noted earlier, the *Mishnah* is the starting point for the discussion of the next generations of sages (called Amoraim) in the land of Israel and Babylonia, from the second century C.E. on. The literary product of these discussions is the Talmud of the land of Israel (called the Jerusalem Talmud) redacted in the mid-fourth century, and the Talmud of Babylonia (called the Babylonian Talmud) redacted with final annotations in the fifth century. These two great collections from the two preeminent centers of Jewish life and scholarship form the next foundation document of developing Judaism. They both gradually achieved the status of authoritative and sacred texts, though only the Babylonian Talmud ever really dominated the academic and legal curriculum of Jewish study over the ages.

Both Talmuds develop the abstract and practical implications of the Tannaitic *Mishnah* (and its supplements), draw inferences about its logic and suppositions, harmonize contradictions among various legal positions (for theoretical and practical purposes), determine the relationship of the *Mishnah* to the Torah legislation, and include an enormous range of legendary, homiletical, and theological matters. The texts preserve the discussions of the sages (as remembered and as reconstructed) in highly compressed and elliptical forms. Accordingly, the Talmuds are enormously difficult to read, and traditional education is geared not only to the contents of the arguments but to the crucial matter of phrasing and sentence division. But because of the supreme importance of these documents for Jewish life and practice, the Talmud (the Amoraic content of which is called *gemara*, "study," though this term is often used generically for the entire Talmudic corpus) has remained the core document of traditional Jewish study. The two Talmuds overlap in almost all the topics dealt with in the second, third, and fourth orders of the *Mishnah*; though the Babylonian Talmud has no discussion on the first division (Seeds), and the Jerusalem Talmud has no discussion on the fifth (Holy Matters). Very little of the Amoraic treatment of the sixth division of the Mishnah (Purities) is preserved.

RABBINIC LITERATURE AND THE TORAH

Faced with such a prodigious intellectual output, one may naturally wonder why such a proliferation was necessary in the first place. The place to begin is with the Bible itself. Despite its divine authority, the rabbis, who wanted to establish a comprehensive biblically based religion, had to deal with the fact that the Torah is not a comprehensive document. Numerous topics necessary for religious-legal life are missing. For example, little or nothing is said in the Torah about the laws of marriage and burial, adoption and contracts, and much more. In addition, where topics are specified in the Torah, they are frequently found to be either ambiguous or in need of supplementation. Thus, for the Torah to be the basis of *all* religious life it was necessary for the sages to make the general rules specific and draw out the implicit meanings of other laws. Because of its overall importance in Jewish life, and as a representative case, let us briefly consider the rules pertaining to Sabbath observance.

The Decalogue, or Ten Commandments, commands the Jew not to work on the Sabbath ("six days shall you labor and do all manner of work; but the seventh day is for the Lord, your God; *you shall not do on it any manner of work* (Exod. 20:9–10; Deut. 5:13–14). But aside from one or two further regulations elsewhere in the Bible (like the prohibition against lighting a fire), the nature of "work" is not specified, so the precise manner of obeying the divine law was left open. It was therefore necessary from early times for teachers to determine a whole host of issues like: *when* the Sabbath day begins (for though new days are reckoned from eventide in Judaism, the strict prohibitions of Sabbath labor required special precision; hence the onset was variously "pushed back" to predusk or earlier); *what* constitutes a forbidden labor (as a formal guide, the thirty-nine Mishnaic rules of prohibited labors in the ancient Temple, like carrying objects and lighting or extinguishing fires, served as precedents); *where* certain of the prohibited Sabbath labors (like carrying objects) applied and where not (complex rules of "boundaries" establishing private vs. public domains were worked out; carrying being permitted in the former); *whether* one could walk beyond certain fixed limits and *in what circumstances* one could break the Sabbath rules for health reasons; and *how* one should comport oneself in demeanor, dress, and thought on the Sabbath day to make it holy and special.

The halakhic discussions of the rabbis on these matters in the Talmud especially are intense and legalistic and filled with great intellectual and theological passion. Gradually a whole complex of rules designed to make the Sabbath "sacred" were formulated or justified through biblical proof-texts. There is thus an overwhelming disproportion between the amount of divine legislation found in the Bible and the amount of human legislation preserved in rabbinic literature. But what is particularly significant about this is that the rabbinc rules are not only designed to help implement the biblical law but *to protect it*. An important legal category thus developed, known as "building a fence around the Torah"; that is, the rabbis typically added many rigorous circumscriptions ("fences") to the biblical law *so that the divine law it protects would not be broken*. The rabbis themselves recognized the ironies involved. According to one early remark found already in the *Mishnah*, the sages stated that the numerous halakhic prescriptions concerned with the proper observance of the Sabbath were like "mountains hanging by a thread." Yet this thread was strong enough to help weave the complex pattern of Jewish holiness and to spin the mysterious web of Jewish continuity. One may therefore concur with the pithy formulation of a later observer: less than the Jews preserved the Sabbath, the Sabbath preserved the Jews.

Now all this may seem an inordinately complex form of religious concern. But it is just this complexity and legal piety that has informed Judaism over the ages. In their concern to establish and obey the positive ("thou shalt") and negative ("thou shalt not") commandments of the Bible with every nuance, and to make certain that rules pertaining to such daily practices as personal hygiene and eating were properly followed, the rabbis and Jews (of these and later times) believed that *in just this way* they were truly faithful to the covenant and God's will on earth. Scrupulous piety, it was hoped, would result in divine blessings in the here and now (what was called *olam hazeh*, "this world"), though the obscurities of fate often led the people to defer this hope to a future time (what was called *olam haba*, "the world to come"). Thus the commandments, or **mitzvot**, were a means of holiness and hope in this world.

The deferral of hope because of historical injustice or the mysteries of divine justice never compromised this mode of holy service. Indeed, for many the "world to come" was no radically transformed existence, but the full earthly realization of the hopes of the Bible: peace on earth, harmony in the family, natural bounty, political dignity (under a native, annointed king, or "**Messiah**"), and restoration of sacrifices (in a rebuilt or heavenly sent Temple). The frustrations of history, especially the abortive national uprising under Bar Kochba (132–135 C.E.), turned many Jews inward, away from issues of political power and toward the spiritual "history" of "the four cubits of the *halakha*," as the concerns of legal piety were sometimes dubbed. The *Mishnah* itself may reflect this very ideology. By contrast, other Jews longed for a radically transformed *olam haba* on earth; or they awaited the manifestation of divine justice in an altogether divine world. Either way, whether rewarded now or later, the unassailable belief and assumption was that the *mitzvot* save, that these "works" are the mysterious means of personal and national salvation, and that they were given by God for just that very purpose.

EXTRALEGAL LITERATURE

The halakhic spirit may thus be summarized as legalistic in its nature, authoritative in its forms, and communal in its sphere of application and performance. A more personal spirit is reflected in the numerous theological interpretations of the Bible known as *midrash aggada.* Coming from the same Tannaitic and Amoraic academies as the legal teachings, the aggadic spirit reflects the theological quest and concerns of the rabbis as reflective interchanges among themselves and as highly stylized sermons delivered to the people on Sabbaths and holidays.

The *aggada* achieves its theological aims through the reapplication of biblical images and themes (e.g., creation or the Exodus), through passionate appeals for repentance and purity of service (i.e., against rote performance of the commandments and self-deception), and through the unrelenting advocation of moral action and personal perfection before God (by reflections on the great biblical models of moral action and religious decision). All this nonlegal material is found in special collections of interpretations of biblical books. Significantly, these aggadic anthologies typically include legal discourses and expositions as well. Similarly, aggadic materials are

Prayer gathering at "Wailing Wall" in Jerusalem, the only remaining portion of the ancient Temple. It has served as a symbol of exile and hope for millennia. Since antiquity this site has been the locus of pilgrimages. Photo credit: Bill Aron.

also woven around the halakhic discussions preserved in the Talmud. This frequent integration of the two types of content is of notable significance. For *halakha* and *aggada* are two sides of Judaism, not just two literary genres, constantly intertwining and mutually challenging. *Halakha* gives the *aggada* its social and public expression; *aggada* gives the *halakha* its spontaneity and extralegal spirit.

In addition to the great ideal of Torah study as a special substitute for the ancient sacrifices, there is another "service of the heart," whereby Judaism replaced and transformed the ancient powers of the Temple. It is the service of the repentant and gracious spirit. One expression of this is a justly celebrated teaching of Rabbi Yochanan ben Zakkai. While many fellow Jews were intensely mourning the loss of the Temple, this sage consoled his students by spiritualizing the meaning of the sacrifices through an adroit reinterpretation of a biblical passage. Picking up a remark of the prophet Hosea, Rabbi Yochanan said that acts of "loving-kindness" replaced and were greater than "sacrifices," and that acts of "repentance" replaced and were greater than "sacrifices of atonement."[7] Loss of the Temple need not, therefore, mean the loss of spiritual renewal and reconciliation with God. This could be achieved, he taught, through pious penitence toward God and personal devotion to one's neighbor. Other sages taught that the commandments themselves might serve as functional substitutes for the ancient sacrifices, insofar as their pious performance was an act of self-sacrifice of personal desire and will. Thus while one might perform the commandments solely as an act of legal piety and thus be considered a *tzaddik*, or just and honorable person, loving devotion to others beyond the strict letter of the law would be the acts of a *hasid*, or righteous person. Such a one goes beyond the needs of the self and sacrifices personal interests for the sake of a higher path of divine service. Such a standard was called the *mishnah* of the righteous, *mishnat hasidim*. It was not the way of the many, but of those who saw it as their concern to enact the reconciliations of the Temple through acts of neighborly devotion. This path had its faithful followers throughout the Middle Ages.

Among the ideals of self-sacrifice of the early sages (preserved and transformed into a national ideal in medieval and modern times by historical necessity), none was greater than martyrdom. In this one act, as Jewish texts repeat, one no longer transfers one's offering to another creature but becomes that very sacrifice. For the rabbis, the patriarch Isaac and the events recorded in Genesis 22 came to constitute the biblical model for this "perfect and unblemished offering"—as midrashic texts speak of his trial on the altar. The story of Isaac was recited daily in the morning liturgy, elaborated upon with much pathos in the *aggada*, and rendered poetically in pious martyrologies throughout the Middle Ages. The great rabbinic scholar Akiba was another model of self-sacrifice for the Jews of classical antiquity and beyond, for during the Hadrianic persecutions (132–135 C.E.), Akiba's flesh was stripped off and hung in the market stalls for disobeying the Roman prohibition of Torah study and observance. According to tradition, his was an awesome display of devotion and piety; he died for the sanctification of God by reciting the proclamation of the unity of God (the Shema) at the climax of his suffering.

One version of the foregoing event of Akiba's martyrdom is preserved in the Talmudic legend of Moses with which we opened this book. After the event in the study hall, when Moses queried God why he and not Akiba should have the merit of receiving the Torah and was abruptly silenced by God ("Be silent, for this is how I have determined it"), Moses asked to see Akiba's fate. Anticipating the reward due the righteous, Moses sees instead the martyrdom of the saint and the shame done to his body. Outraged, Moses exclaims, "This is Torah, and this its reward?!" Is *this* the result of a life devoted to Torah study and piety? Just as abruptly as before, God silences Moses and says, "Be silent, for this is how I have determined it." No further answer is given. The two scenes of the Talmudic account—of devoted study and ultimate faithfulness to God and His law—conjointly express the deepest ideals and ideology of Jews in this classical period: that Jewish renewal is achieved through devoted interpretation of Moses' Torah and that Jewish destiny is fatefully bound up with its ongoing life of Torah. Or, to reexpress the matter in the folk adage quoted earlier, "Israel and the Torah are one."

The Amoraic period ended in the land of Israel about 425 C.E. with the abolition of the Patriarchate by the Roman emperor Theodosius II. It was brought to a close in Babylonia about a century later, after persecutions of the Jews by the Sassanians. By that time the seat of the Jewish religious authority had long since shifted to the Babylonian Exilarch (as the leader of the Jewish community there was called) and to the great Babylonian academies established in the cities of Sura, Pumbedita, and Nehardea. It was here that such rabbinic authorities as Rab and Samuel left their mark on Jewish legal theory and literature for all time, as did the later pair of sages Abbaye and Rava. Through the efforts of these scholars, the rabbis of the Pharaisaic tradition suceeded in establishing their legal and moral authority over most of the house of Israel.

Developments in Judaism from the Seventh Through the Seventeenth Centuries

We have paused at some length to discuss the ideological system of Judaism during its formative phase (from 70 C.E. to the redaction of the two Talmuds) for three reasons. First, while Judaism changed in its emphases over succeeding centuries, the Tannaitic-Amoraic period of the religion is its classical expression and brings to focus the essential features of Judaism that dominated Jewish life for the next thousand years. That is, *the core features of the classical phase remained the matrix of traditional Jewish life*: Torah study and interpretation; legal piety through fulfillment of the commandments; human responsibility before God and God's responsiveness to human action and need; and the chosenness of Israel among the nations along with the hope in the eventual unification of all peoples in a just and righteous order.

The second reason for this emphasis on the formative phase of Judaism is that its core features were repeated daily by all Jews in the formulations of the liturgy. That is, *the ideological features of the classical phase were continuously reactivated in Jewish consciousness through the liturgy and its behaviors.* And finally, the theological and legal texts of classical Judaism became the agenda for subsequent Jewish speculation and interpretation. That is, *the halakhic and aggadic expressions of the formative phase were the basis for ongoing Jewish creativity and expression.*

With all this in mind, we shall now see at somewhat greater length how the classical rabbinic inheritance was variously complicated, consolidated, elaborated, and explained in the postclassical period.

ISRAEL

Already after the first exile (587/6 B.C.E.), the Jews were a dispersed nation subject to diverse national and religious influences. This remained so in the classical phase, when the two dominant centers were the land of Israel and Babylonia (with their Greco-Roman and Irano-Sassanian influences, respectively), and continued to characterize Jewish life in the Middle Ages. Gradually these two centers fell under the influence of Christianity and Islam and their temporal religious heads in Rome and Baghdad. As Jewish life fanned out from Israel to Spain and Morocco in the west, and to Iraq and Persia in the east, the Jewish cultural styles of these environments (known as **Ashkenazi** in Franco-Germany and Italy, and as **Sephardi** in Spain and the Near East) were continuously affected by their Christian and Islamic overlords. Inevitably, for all classes, these influences included participation in the regional dialect and folk repertoire and the more subtle factors of aesthetic taste and demeanor. Among the mercantile and scholarly classes, the influences extended to shared legal and economic conventions and common intellectual and literary interests.

Nevertheless, within this wider framework, the Jews carved out (at the discretion of the popes and princes of the church, and the sultans and imams of the mosque, to be sure) their own autonomous (if largely second-class) culture. Here, in the Jewish domain, Ashkenazi and Sephardi communities developed their own linguistic jargon (like Yiddish, a mixture of Hebrew, German, and Slavic elements; or Ladino, a mixture of Hebrew, old Spanish, and Provencal elements); their own folk heritage and art forms; and their own distinctive mores and styles of family life. And here, too, in the autonomous Jewish domains, the rabbinic lawyers (and their courts and halakhic rules) held sway. Issues of religious concern (like prayer and food slaughter) were subject to Jewish authority, while issues of public status (like taxation and state service) and public behavior (like expressed support of the state and its leaders) were subject to external, non-Jewish authority. In the context of an often precarious balance between rights obtained and negotiated, Jews lived in separate enclaves where they established synagogues for prayer, academies for study, and whole networks for communal services (like care for the sick and poor; or burial and aid societies) in all the lands of their settlement. Naturally, the communal patterns changed according to region and time; and they also varied in degrees of political or economic efficiency. But all told, Jewish self-government and accompanying bureaucracies were a reality throughout the Middle Ages and a reality the Jews depended upon for their support and safety.

Thus if the Jews found themselves dispersed abroad, they were nevertheless centralized within their local communities, often called "the holy community" of this city or that. And if, further, the Jews in Muslim lands were categorized as *dhimmis* (Arab.; i.e., non-Muslims formally protected by a "pact" with Muslim overlords), who were at best tolerated when not completely harassed, and the Jews of Christian Europe were totally outside the law and thoroughly dependent upon benign papal bulls and the goodwill of local electors (the Jews were called Lat., *servi camerae*, "servants of the royal chamber"), they still maintained their belief to be God's chosen people. The principle of *ahavat Yisrael*, the love and care for fellow Jews, was a central value for this oppressed minority, as was the principle that stated that "all Jews are responsible for one another." In normal times, where communal and intercommunal self-help was required, these principles were often the motivations for social kindness. During times of danger and oppression, these principles also motivated Jews to rescue merchants frequently kidnapped for high ransom, to defend their compatriots against frequent Christian blood libels (which outrageously imputed that Jews murdered Christian children to use their blood in their Passover holiday bread or that they "tormented" the blood and body of Jesus through desecrations of the Eucharist host and wine), and to provide a safe haven and care for Jews exiled from one city and country to another.

Overall, Jewish literature and historical memory in the Middle Ages is a traumatized memory of "tears and martyrdom," as one historian put it, of national-cultural destructions that turned whole communities into rivers of blood or torrents of homeless exiles. Years like 1096, when the Jews of the Rhineland were plundered and killed by Christian pilgrims on their circuitous crusade to liberate Jerusalem, and 1648–49, when hundreds of thousands of Jews were butchered by the Cossak chieftain Chmielnitzki and his hordes during Ukranian uprisings, are deeply etched in the collective memory of the Jews. Equally cataclysmic are such dates as 1290, 1306, 1391, 1395, 1492, and 1497, times when Jews were expelled from England, France, Spain, and Portugal. Many more dates could be added. No wonder that the Jews of medieval Europe rarely regarded themselves as part of the history of the gentile nations. Theirs, they believed, was a sacred history politically disrupted in 70 C.E. but to revived again in the ever-near messianic future.

The focus of the people of Israel was thus neither politics nor power, but the maintenance of their halakhic patterns and the time-transcending demands of a comprehensive religious tradition. In this regard, Gentiles were treated with outward civil respect but inner suspicion and reserve, for the inescapable fact is that Jewish history in Christian Europe and the Muslim lands was a nightmare for medieval Jews, the ever-present confirmation of their life in **galut**, or exile. On the other hand, the messianic longing for redemption, outbreaks of which recurred repeatedly from the seventh century in Yemen to the seventeenth century in Europe and the Near East, reflects the deep Jewish passions for a restoration of their national dignity and the right to perform their religion freely.

These powerful messianic passions were fanned daily by the texts of the liturgy as well as by the pervasive Jewish belief—against all outward logic—that Jewish history was providentially guided by God and was thus ultimately subject to no temporal power. And so, while the outward course of history appeared under the bleak image

A Sabbath examination of pupil by elders in the eastern European manner (turn of century America, ca. 1901). Students were traditionally responsible to parents for the week's "learning." Photo courtesy of American Jewish Historical Society.

of the "eternal Jew" wandering from one burning city to another, Jews as a whole held fast to a more inward course of history, a history believed to be a meaningful and God-directed affair within which the Jews played a pivotal role. No understanding of Judaism or Jewish historical resilience in the Middle Ages can begin or end without taking this belief into account.

HALAKHA

Halakhic piety served to provide Jews with a special and autonomous life pattern and a buffer against political harassment and theological attack. It also provided *the consensus* for Jewish life the world over. Jews wandering from one land to another could easily adapt to the new environments because of the common calendar, common rituals, common sacred objects, and, especially, common legal norms. The latter grew out of the Talmudic traditions and expanded during the Middle Ages, first by the Geonim, the "Excellencies" or heads of the Babylonian academies from the seventh to the eleventh centuries (until the fall of the Baghdad Califate), and later by the Rishonim, the "Earlier Authorities," from the twelfth through the sixteenth centuries. The scattered and diverse halahkic norms were variously compiled by such scholars as Yehudai Gaon, in his eighth-century collection *Halakhot Pesukot*; by Simeon Kayyara, in his ninth-century collection *Halakhot Gedolot*; by Rabbi Isaac Alfasi (known by the acronym Rif), in his eleventh-century collection *Sefer ha-Halakhot*; by the extremely influencial works of Rabbi Moses **Maimonides** (known by the acronym Rambam), in his thirteenth-century work *Mishneh Torah*; by Rabbi Jacob ben Asher, in his fourteenth-century codification *Turim* (known as "The Tur"); and by Rabbi Joseph Karo, in his sixteenth-century work *Shulkhan Arukh*. All these works are justly famous in Jewish life; they gave a systematic structure to Jewish legal piety over the ages. Some medieval scholars complained that the works of Maimonides and Karo, especially, formulated as they were without citing precedents of legal reasoning, tended to give Jews the impression of a fixed and apodictic legal system. This was not an altogether unjust complaint—especially as far as Jews with minimal rabbinic training were concerned. But the elaborate "Question and Answer" literature (called *Responsa*) from early Geonic times, in which new halakhic queries and their solutions were constantly being discussed, belie this impression of halakhic rigidity. This literature (and the process of discussion and reasoning involved) remains a window to the passions and perplexities of halakhic life to this day.

The halakhic consensus of traditional Jewish life also established the centrality of the rabbis as local lawyers and judges and as communal leaders and teachers of God's law. Faced with the fact that their legal reasoning was interpretative in nature, the rabbis sought to establish the legitimacy of their methods and conclusions by recording chains of authorities—something like spiritual-religious genealogies (comparable to the Islamic *isnads* or Buddhist lists of teachers). This concern was also motivated by the Karaite challenge from the seventh century on. This group, founded by one Anan ben David, rejected "Rabbinite" authority and halakhic reasoning and sought to develop its own "biblical" religion (the word "Karaite" derives from the nouns *mikra* or *kera*, as Scripture was called). They exhorted their followers to "search the Scriptures well," and to use natural reason and logic—not rabbinic exegesis—in developing new legal norms and rules from the Bible. The basis for this lay in the Karaite contention that the interpretative procedures of Talmudic antiquity distorted the meaning and application of the divine Law.

Despite the power and pervasiveness of the Rabbinite establishment, the Karaite challenge was strong and serious and frequently split the Jewish community into bitter factions for centuries. The great Gaons (or "Excellencies"), like Saadia of Sura, frequently debated the contentions of the Karaites, while many other rabbis used every opportunity to criticize the Karaites' calendrical calculations and their often literalist legal interpretations. Ostensibly, the issue was a concern for a halakhic consensus among all Jews and the "proper" interpretation of the divine law, but the desire for power and control over the Jewish populace cannot be excluded as a motivation. By the high Middle Ages (thirteenth–fifteenth centuries), the vituperative debates slackened somewhat, and the Karaites settled into enclaves with their own hegemony in such areas as Constantinople and northwestern and southern Russia. The remnants of this Jewish community were sought out and killed, along with other Jews, during World War II.

The halakhic work of the rabbis reinforced and further extended the dimensions of Jewish legal piety. Every sphere of personal and communal life was regulated by it. But this was hardly abstract law, for as we have seen, the *mitzvot*—the visible expressions of *halakha*—were the commandments of God (as rabbinically formulated) that established the religious (not just legal) basis for life. Through performance of the *mitzvot* the Jew was constantly in relation to God, constantly sanctifying life by holy actions, and constantly accruing "merits" for future (earthly or otherworldly) blessedness. Thus, through the *mitzvot* life remained centered on earthly actions *even as* these commandments were simultaneously directed toward God, their source. It is characteristic of Jewish legal piety that the very codes that established halakhic order are also pervaded by great religious devotion. The Sephardic sage Moses Maimonides (author of the *Mishneh Torah*) and his Ashkenazi contemporary Rabbi Elazar of Worms (author of the *Rokeach*) both begin their important works with spiritually passionate sections dealing with the ideals of Torah study and its deep connection to the love of God and moral-religious perfection (through the *mitzvot*). "Arise like a lion, run like a deer, to fulfill the commandment of the Creator," charges Joseph Karo at the beginning of his own great legal code (the *Shulkhan Arukh*).

BIBLE STUDY

As is understandable, a great deal of halakhic study was practical in nature (*halakha le-ma'aseh*, as it was called), for Jewish piety had to be defined, applied, and judged. At the same time, already in many Talmudic discussions and increasingly among the Franco-German "glossators" (called Tosaphists) and others, the concern for halakhic theory was prevalent—the natural process of law being the establishment of theoretical structures and the discussion of theoretical cases. But it should be noted that from the last stages of the Talmud on, in addition to trends toward more theoretical analysis, halakhic issues moved increasingly away from the Bible and focused on Tannaitic-Amoraic discourses (harmonizing them or reframing their concerns) as well as the subsequent formulations of the Geonim. The dependence of the rabbis upon rabbinic literature was certainly part of the Karaite critique, which, it will be recalled, urged a return to biblical foundations. While the rabbis did not restructure their halakhic reasoning on this account, they did return to Bible study in a new way.

The first new activity that must be mentioned is the work of the Massoretes. It is they who studied and annotated the biblical text. They were concerned that its letters and vowels along with its reading signs and oddities were preserved intact—for the sake of an exact tradition (the very name Massoretes, which means something like "traditioners," reflects this concern). The Massoretes collated Bible manuscripts, collated textual variants, and also noted linguistic idosyncracies or parallels in the texts. Their work seem to have begun around the seventh or eighth century and hit a highwater mark in the ninth and tenth centuries, though it continued for hundreds of years thereafter. The Massoretes established the traditional text of the Bible through their great compilations, and many of their remarks can be found in the margins or in sections following particular books in the so-called Rabbinic Bibles, *Mikra'ot Gedolot*, printed beginning in the sixteenth century and continuing up to today.

One of the hallmarks of the Rabbinic Bible is the inclusion in it of some of the popular or preeminent Jewish medieval commentators. Indeed, one of the special features of the work of these rabbis is their concern for the "plain sense" of the biblical text. In its earliest forms, this plain sense (called *peshat*) was not so easily distinguished from rabbinic modes of interpretation (called *derash*). In fact, the great early commentator of eleventh-century France, Rabbi Solomon ben Isaac (known by the acronym **Rashi**), who first set forth the program of a *peshat* commentary on the Bible, often slips into the mode of *derash* to support a narrative or legal point. Nevertheless, the very attempt to establish a working cultural distinction between something that would resemble the explicative and historical sense of the biblical text (the *peshat*), on the one hand, and the midrashic sense of the text (legal and theological *derash*), on the other, was of considerable importance for Jewish and Christian Bible studies. Other commentators soon elaborated upon this exegetical dichotomy. Among these was Rashi's own grandson, Rabbi Samuel ben Meier (known by the acronym Rashbam) of the eleventh–twelfth centuries. Indeed, he maintained a vigorous concern for the linguistic-historical sense of the Bible. In pursuing the sense of *peshat*, in fact, Rashbam even interpreted the Bible against the sense of the halakhic tradition (the *derash*). Presumably for Rashbam, and not for him alone, the Bible was believed to contain both senses in a noncontradictory way, though of course the midrashic sense was authoritative for halakhic behavior. It appears that pressures from outside Judaism (specifically, new Christian arguments and contentions) lie at the root of this new rabbinic interest in the *peshat* of Scripture.

The concern to penetrate the *peshat* of Scripture gradually became a Jewish scholarly concern in its own right. For the rabbinic scholars in Spain, this textual interest was further accelerated by growing developments in philology in the contemporary Islamic world. Among the notable new voices was that of Rabbi Abraham ibn Ezra in the twelfth century. In the introduction to his Bible commentary, he aggressively separated the different styles and interests of contemporary Bible commentators and opted for the plain, grammatical-historical sense of the text. Ibn Ezra's work is marked by a high literary style and a pithy acuity that set generations of students to work to discern the exact sense of his comments (such annotations are known as supercommentaries). Many other scholars of this period, like Rabbis Joseph and David Kimhi of Narbonne, Rabbi Eliezar of Beaugency, and Joseph Chicatilla, labored to establish the method of *peshat* interpretation.

The important Bible commentary of the twelfth–thirteenth century Sephardic scholar Rabbi Moses ben Nachman (also called Nachmanides and known by the acronym Ramban) is more complex and synthetic than the preceding works. For one thing, he takes up and debates the earlier comments of the classical sages, of Rashi and ibn Ezra, though almost invariably providing a distinctive approach to the plain sense of a scriptural passage. However, Ramban was also a devoted traditionalist and important halakhist, and he turns his comments in that direction where matters of law or practice are concerned. Thus, though Ramban clearly saw it as the task of the Bible commentator to serve theoretical and scholarly interests, he also felt it to be his responsibility to write a work that would serve the religious community in its faith and practice. This helps explain another particular element in his Bible commentary: his mystical allusions. While he indicates his strong mystical concerns in his introduction (and his belief that the *peshat* hardly exhausts the meaning or truth of the Torah), Ramban was exceedingly careful not to be too explicit about these matters in a public commentary (as per rabbinic doctrine). He therefore often closes a cryptic mystical observation with the caveat "but the discerning one will understand" or "we have no (mystical) tradition on this."

By contrast with these various philological and mystical interests, the values of Renaissance humanism also penetrated into Jewish Bible commentaries. The voluminous work of the courtier Don Isaac Abarbanel (Spain and Italy; sixteenth century) typifies this trend, for here we have at once a highly systematic synthesis of the preceding centuries of Spanish exegesis as well as original literary and historical observations. At several points Abarbanel even includes elements characteristic of late Renaissance statecraft and political theory.

In all, this and the preceding works of scriptural interpretation provided many new insights into the text. Most significantly, much of this labor served to restore to Jews the study of the Bible as a document in its own right—neither as a source of *halakha* nor a repository of mystical symbols, but as a work whose very language, rhetoric, and logic was of cultural value. Perhaps one may perceive in this threefold interest an echo of the older medieval scholarly curriculum (the Latin *trivium*) within the study halls of the Jews.

THEOLOGY

The native theology of traditional Judaism is a biblical theology, a theology rooted in biblical images and ideas, in biblical language and hopes, and in biblical values and concerns, however much these images, hopes, and values were transformed through reinterpretation and reformulation. Being so biblically based, much of the ancient and early medieval theology is preserved in the books of *midrash aggada* spoken about earlier (i.e., in commentaries on biblical books and homilies on Torah readings and holiday themes). For this reason, too, the themes and topics of this early theology are not systematized under any abstract heading but follow the sequence of biblical texts and the lead of their topics: God, the creation, the patriarchs, Moses, the covenant, the homeland, kingship, and so on. Invariably, a particular verse sequence and its imagery elicit many other scriptural texts with similar or contrasting language or ideas. These are then coordinated with the biblical passage that initiates the aggadic reflection. The result is a vast web of ideas from the entirety of Scripture. Aggadic theology is therefore a total biblical theology; and because it is such, its images of God are anthropomorphic (i.e., God sees and speaks, loves and judges, and so on), not abstract; and its views on any given topic are as varied and contradictory as is the entire biblical inheritance. This bothered no one and actually gave Jewish theological life a nondogmatic flexibility—within the broad constraints of Judaism's "essential features," to be sure, and the more narrow limits of halakhic conformity.

Those medieval theologies like Judah Halevi's *Kuzari: Defense of a Despised Faith* (twelfth century, Spain), which retained the pathos of the living and guiding God of Abraham and Moses and did not neutralize this pathos through abstract philosophical analysis, thus remained true to the native theology of Judaism and captured the hearts of the Jewish populace. Little wonder, then, that Halevi was the great "sweet singer of Israel" in the Middle Ages, whose religious (and biblically rooted) poetry entered the prayer book of the Jews.

> Lord, where shall I find You?
> High and hidden is Your place.
> And where shall I not find You?
> The world is filled with Your Glory.

> I have sought Your nearness,
> With all my heart I have called You;
> And going out to meet You,
> I found You coming toward me.[8]

With these words Halevi speaks for all traditional Jews, of a God utterly exalted and hidden, but of a Presence also near and immediate. He speaks of the passions of religious yearning and the mystery of God's kingship, but also of the joy expressing the certainty that God responds to his creatures in love. This, too, is the biblical and rabbinic God of light and power, who also "clothes the naked" and "raises the downtrodden." Such a God is deemed a living Father and King, the revealer of covenant demands and promises; and he is also the One who is trusted to redeem his people and restore them to their ancestral homeland, to Zion. Of this longing for national redemption Halevi says: "My heart is in the east/and I am at the edge of the west." And with the melancholy of his entire nation, the poet cries to Zion: "I am like a jackal when I weep for your affliction; but when I dream of/the return of your exiles, I am a lute for your songs."9 Similar hopes and longings were recited daily in the prayer service, as was the acknowledgement of God the Creator, who has chosen his people in love and revealed to them his teachings for their holiness and ultimate salvation.

More systematic, philosophical expressions of Jewish theology were introduced into Judaism during the course of its encounters with Islamic and Greek philosophy in the Middle Ages. The range of topics did not change from that found in the *aggada* or liturgy (God, Israel, covenant, Torah, and messianic hope); but much of the native pathos was neutralized by the rational and abstract tone of the philosophers. Typical of such efforts and of monumental significance for the history of Jewish thought is the philosophical work of Moses Maimonides, who was mentioned above as the author of one of Jewry's most influential legal codes. In his great work, *The Guide of the Perplexed*, Maimonides gave paramount importance to his philosophical reading of the ancient biblical tradition, though he conceded the value—even necessity—of a more naive and literalist understanding of Scripture for most Jews. In this way, he argued, those persons not capable of abstract philosophical analysis might nevertheless be guided on the way of truth through a reliance upon the concrete and anthropomorphic imagery of the Bible. Naturally, for him the philosophical approach was the higher and more individualistic way to truth. But the important point was that the seemingly naive biblical tradition was not therefore to be rejected: it was a necessary, though not final, level of meaning, the public expression, in fact, of God's revelation of Mount Sinai. Thus ordinary people had immediate access to divine truth through the revelation and subsequent rabbinic explanations of it, whereas the philosopher added the more arduous path of intellect and logical argument. Despite this high privilege accorded to philosophical reason, Maimonides nevertheless conceded that, without the biblical view of God as Creator in time (that is, not an Abstract Idea out of time), the whole foundation of Judaism—based on God's revelation and teachings, on divine guidance and redemption—would crumble.

A complex balance between reason and revealed truth was therefore a philosophical necessity. It is thus notable that when Maimonides formulated his "Thirteen Principles of Faith," he combined the abstract language and arrangement of the philosopher with the content of a living, biblical theology. This creedal statement, preserved in the daily prayer book, states: "I believe, in perfect faith, that the Creator, may His Name be blessed" is (1) the sole Creator, (2) uniquely One, (3) beyond all conception and form, (4) the First and the Last, and (5) the true God of prayer; that, further, (6) the words of the prophets are True, that (7) Moses is the True and First prophet, and that (8) the whole Torah was given to Moses; moreover, that (9) there is no new covenant; that (10) the Creator is Omniscient and (11) rewards and punishes for observance of the commandments; and further, that (12) in his own time God will yet bring the Messiah, and (13) resurrect the dead. A discerning review of this formulation will perceive both the abiding theological matrix of traditional Judaism *and* the outright rejection of the principles of Muslim and Christian belief (note numbers 2–3, 5–9, and 12).

ETHICS

The sphere of halakhic action has two main foci: ritual actions performed between the individual and God (*bein adam la-Makom*), and moral actions performed between one individual and another (*bein adam le-havero*). The first sphere includes prayer, physical purity, proper dietary regulations, and celebrations of the festivals; the second includes legal actions, business transactions, respect for parents, and the obligation to marry off children and bury the dead. Both spheres are governed by the *halakha*, in the sense that strict norms of performance and behavior are imposed upon the Jew; and the actions in both spheres are *mitzvot*, in the sense that they are ultimately derived from the Bible and performed in the service of God. In Judaism, then, ethical action is part of halakhic action and done with God in mind. It is just this double character of regulated interpersonal actions done for the glory of God that is the touchstone of traditional Jewish ethics.

Native Jewish ethics derive from the Bible and the whole library of aggadic literature. As with theology, the reflections on actions and duties, or motivations and ideal behavior, arise in the course of reflecting upon biblical actions. How the patriarchs acted, the dangers of pride and the value of penitence, and the duties to the "stranger,

orphan, and widow" are among the biblical topics taken up in the
midrash aggada. To be sure, the classical rabbinic literature does
show some trends toward a more systematic collection of ethical actions. The Tannaitic treatise *Sayings of the Fathers*, for example,
gathers together some ethical dicta of the early sages, and a hierarchical list of spiritual perfections has been preserved in the Talmud
in the name of Phineas ben Yair.

Despite these trends toward systematization in the classical
sources, traditional ethical behaviors and motivations were only
gradually gathered and ordered in the post-Talmudic period. Soon a
voluminous literature developed. The ethical work of Bahya ibn Pa-
kuda (Spain, eleventh century) is a crucial turning point in this regard. His influential *Duties of the Heart* deliberately shifts focus
from the outer, halakhic level of behavior (the "duties of the
limbs") to the inner sphere of motivation and self-scrutiny (the
"duties of the heart"). In an elegant and enticing way, this work
guides the reader along an ideal path of perfection from proper belief in God, to the virtues of trust, sincerity, penitence, semi-asceti-
cism, and fear and love of God, all in the context of discussing the
traditional halakhic actions and their proper motivation. Bahya's
Duties was of immense importance in medieval Europe and was de-
votedly studied by pietist circles from the Rhineland (the German
Hasidim, twelfth–thirteenth centuries) to the Ukraine (the so-called
new Hasidim, from the eighteenth century).

Other influential works like Rabbi Jonah Gerondi's *Gates of Re-
pentence* (thirteenth century, Spain), or Rabbi Elijah de Vidas's *Beginning of Wisdom* (land of Israel, sixteenth century), or Rabbi Moses Luzzatto's *Path of the Upright* (Italy, eighteenth century) further
directed the Jew toward holiness, self-purification, and unselfish actions. Most literate homes had some *musar* (ethical) books or pamphlets in their libraries. In their content and ideal value, then, these
holy handbooks are to be considered central to appreciating the
ever-renewed quest of Jewish spiritual life for devoting all actions to
God alone. It was, in addition, a literature of the traditional community at large and did not require highly developed rabbinic skills
for its comprehension.

By contrast, the philosophical ethical literature, which also derives
from a biblical foundation, was written with elites in mind and was
greatly influenced by ancient Greek ethical systems. Many of these

works, like Solomon ibn Gabirol's *Perfection of the Qualities of the Soul* (eleventh century, Spain), linked Greek psychological theories to theories of ethical development. The several structures of the human soul (the so-called corporeal, divine, and supernal elements) were systematically related to the structures of ethical and spiritual development. Thus, one's actions might move from lesser to increasingly more refined instincts, and from there to higher intentions—like uniting one's highest soul element to God. The even "purer" philosophical ethics of Maimonides were also based upon biblical passages and Talmudic sayings as well as ancient and medieval psychological theories. But it is also very much distinguished by the influence of Aristotle's *Nichomachian Ethics*. The result is Greek ethics in a Jewish guise. It is chiefly when he is providing moral-spiritual explanations to the practical laws (as in the *Book of Knowledge* of the *Mishneh Torah*) or ordering the normative way of giving charity or doing repentance from rabbinic sources that Maimonides' ethics are distinctly characterized by biblical-rabbinic language and values. It is, further, in just this area of his work that the ancient Jewish passion for *religious perfection in and through society* is most clear.

Rabbinic Patterns of Hidden Meanings and Otherworldly Concerns

The patterns of rabbinic life and thought that were considered in the preceding section under the rubric of "this-worldly holiness and salvation," may be referred to as the exoteric or public level of Judaism. This level is rooted in the public nature of the biblical revelation and the social context of the commandments. Referring to the accessibility of the Torah, Moses reminds the people that this teaching "is not in heaven," for "the hidden things are God's, but the revealed things are for us and our children forever: to do all the teachings of the Torah (Deut. 29:28). Thus through the *mitzvot* and the *halakha*, the public, earthly nature of divine service is never lost in Judaism. The mitzvot are works done in this world and for the sake of this world. Moreover, through these earthly works people can relate to God, who is the source of the *mitzvot*. This world is thus the enduring context of holiness and of religious experience and expression, according to standard Jewish teaching.

Nevertheless, a distinct esoteric or hidden level of meaning is evident in Judaism over the ages, not particularly in the sense that special knowledge or secrets are withheld from the people-at-large (though this was sometimes the case), but in the sense that the texts and works of Judaism were believed to contain deeper and more hidden levels of meaning. And, indeed, precisely these deeper levels of meaning should be the true focus of the adept. The esotericists would thus interpret the foregoing Deuteronomic passage to mean that God's Torah contains *both* hidden and public meanings and that the former may be discerned by the adepts either through rational deduction (the way of philosophy) or spiritual disclosure (the way of mysticism). The esoteric trend is thus an elitist phenomenon that focuses on the individual and the special wisdom to be found in the Torah. It builds upon, but does not reject, the populist trend, which focuses on the halakhic consensus founded upon the Torah.

In what follows we shall not review each of the main periods of Jewish life from the detailed perspective of Jewish esotericism and its otherworldly meanings and concerns. Rather, a more selected focus shall be offered of the major historical types found in the philosophical and mystical approaches to Judaism. The ancient dictum that the world is founded upon "Torah, worship, and acts of lovingkindness" will have its echoes in the present review as well.

The Philosophical Path

The dominant image for this path may be "apples of gold set in silver traceries." It is an image made famous by Maimonides in the introduction to his monumental philosophical work, *The Guide of the Perplexed*. Commenting on the biblical adage that "A word fitly spoken is like apples of gold in settings of silver" (Prov. 25:11), Maimonides speaks of discerning the truth of Torah. For one who simply looks at Scripture at a distance, without close examination, the inner truth of the text is misperceived for its outer expressions, just like one looking "with imperfect attention" at golden apples around which silver filigree has been traced might imagine that these apples were solely silver. Only "with full attention" will the interior become clear to the viewer, and he or she will know the apples to be of pure gold.[10] Thus one must penetrate beyond the surface sense of Scripture, for while its external expressions are "useful for beliefs concerned with truth," they cover "truth as it is." The uncovering of the deeper sense of Scripture, of Torah, is through allegory.

Faced with the abstract and sophisticated philosophical view of God taught in the Hellenist schools, Philo of Alexandria (20 B.C.E.–50 C.E.), as remarked earlier, was concerned to show that the Torah, revealed Truth, was, despite its external imagery and anthropomorphic portrait of God, in accord with philosophical truth and reason. Through a complex retranslation of biblical imagery into Greek categories and a reinterpretation of the great personalities of the Bible in terms of Platonic and Stoic virtues, Philo claimed to penetrate to the "deep sense" of Scripture—its philosophical truth. Thus while he emphasized that this deeper level of the Bible—which the rabbis were to call *remez*—did not displace the *peshat* (plain sense) of Scripture or the halakhic actions based on rabbinic *derash*, his intellectual energy was nevertheless focused on philosophical concerns and the "intellectual love" of God. For him, Torah was no mere book of narratives portraying human virtues or vices and its view of God was not mere anthropomorphic presentation of a loving or wrathful diety. Rather, when rightly read, the Bible was nothing less than a divinely given handbook of philosophical truths.

Philo taught that the Bible as a revealed work of wisdom is replete with instructions concerned with guiding one to moral-intellectual perfection. Such instructions occur in the narratives, the laws, and the exhortations. For example, the constant human struggle between the rational and irrational parts of the psyche is for Philo symbolized in the Bible by the raising and lowering of Moses' arms in the battle against Amalek (Exod. 17). Or further, the ancient Greek theme of the soul's exile from its true divine homeland and its struggle to remove itself from the material world through a life of moral-intellectual perfection is particularly symbolized by the lives of the patriarchs. Accordingly, when Scripture reports that "the Lord said to Abraham: 'Go forth from your homeland, your kin and your father's house,' " the hidden instruction to us is the necessity to disengage from the body, sense perception, and speech (i.e., the illusions and attractions of language) in order to draw close to God, the truly "existent One," through contemplation. So guided by Scripture, Jews may live philosophically within their tradition. Far from turn-

ing them from philosophy, Philo taught, the proper study of the
Bible is a philosophical exercise, for philosophical truths are contained *within* it.

Maimonides continued this ancient allegorical-intellectual tradition and provided its classical medieval expression. Concerned with
demonstrating the true philosophical sense of the Bible and purify-
ing the text from its anthropomorphic images of God, Maimonides
began his *Guide* with a virtual philosophical dictionary. Hereby, one
anthropomorphic image after another is explained—and in effect
explained away. Thus, though the language of the text may appear
to indicate that God sees and talks and so on or that he has eyes and
hands, these images are reinterpreted in more abstract categories.
What the text "really means" is that God is omniscient, omnipo-
tent, providential, and so on. In this way the cruder features of the
Bible are refined, as it were.

Now all this does not mean that the outer form of the Bible is
false and an offense against reason. Recalling the opening image of
golden apples, what this rather means is that this exterior level is *also*
part of the sense and truth of the biblical text—deliberately produced by God, says Maimonides, to enable common people to appreciate (via the metaphors and concrete language) the power and
beneficence of God. So impressed, they will undertake the performance of the commandments and thus be guided to moral-social
perfection. Were the biblical text merely philosophical in rigor and
rhetoric, were it merely abstract and logical, Maimonides contended,
God's teachings would have been restricted to the intellectual elite.
In their present form, by contrast, the entire nation is guided to perfection and true belief, each according to his or her intellectual abili-
ties and needs.

For Maimonides, then, Scripture is constituted by truth at its exterior and deeper levels. The latter contains what are often called the
sitre torah, or esoteric "mysteries of the Torah" (such matters as the
true nature of God, metaphysics, and the divine realm as well as the
true meaning of the biblical narratives and the purposes of the positive and negative commandments). Hence the Bible is a teaching for
both the ordinary believer and the philosopher, who will be more
perplexed by the surface formulations of Scripture and more in need
of expert guidance—lest skepticism and rejection of religion result.
"A person ignorant of the secret meaning of Scripture and the deep-

er significance of the law" might thus tend to misperceive the special wisdom of Judaism and be subject to doubts or loss of faith. For this reason, Maimonides believed, it is necessary to enhance this deeper knowledge—for the ordinary folk and the intellectual elite—in different ways. And this he did through the moral-spiritual explanations of the laws found in the *Mishneh Torah* and through the more penetrating interpretations of action and belief found in the *Guide*. Special effort is therefore made to teach the deeper philosophical sense of God and the Torah through philosophical emphases and allegorical reinterpretation. And a special effort is also made to inculcate the deeper sense of the *mitzvot* through an explication of the higher moral and religious ends they serve.

Thus, teaches Maimonides, God, being utterly beyond human description, can only be thought of negatively, by considering what he is not; and being utterly perfect and One, God can hardly be thought of through the compound features of language. By taking care in this regard, one will therefore refine one's religious sensibility and be guided to a purer and more devoted divine service. The language one uses about God is thus directly related, for Maimonides, to the way one conceives of the meaning or motivation of human action. Crass views of God, he judged, would lead to crass and self-centered expectations of personal benefit when performing the *mitzvot*, whereas a more philosophically purified perception of God would lead to a more spiritual and God-directed form of observance. Remarking on the commandments, he further observed: "Know that all the practices of worship, such as reading the Torah, prayer and the performance of the commandments have only the end of training you to occupy yourself with His commandments."[11] But, he continues, if your attention is weak and "you pray merely by moving your lips," or "read the Torah with your tongue while your heart is set" on personal matters, or "you perform a commandment merely with your limbs," such worship is a perfunctory and self-centered act.[12] By such rote behavior true love of God is not achieved, and the perfections of Torah are abused. One of the concerns of philosophical wisdom was, therefore, to challenge and readdress religious routinization through the proper comprehension of the nature of God and the goal of the commandments.

Still, it must be stressed, the path of philosophy was precarious and not for all comers. The weak-minded could easily be befuddled.

For example, if God in the philosophical understanding is pure Intellect or Thought, one might naturally wonder how he is also the concerned revealer of Torah and the caring protector of Israel. Or further, if God is conceived of as a pure Unity and utterly Impassable, one could naturally imagine that such a God was not one to whom prayer and supplications might be addressed. In this light, some interpreters have argued that Maimonides was himself caught on the horns of this apparent series of contradictions and was really a philosopher who advocated religion for the welfare and perfection of humankind. Others have contended that Maimonides skillfully integrated the two modes of philosophy and religion and that for him the paths were thoroughly complementary—though on different levels.

Such speculations transcend the merely academic and have had serious practical consequences. For example, shortly after the publication of Maimonides' *Guide* the rabbis in France and Germany provoked a bitter controversy over its contents. It was their conviction that only a belief in the biblical-rabbinic God was faithful to Judaism and would ensure Jewish practice. Philosophical reinterpretations of Judaism, they believed, obscured the pathos and demands of the God of the covenant, and rather than being a means toward the purification of belief and practice were rather the alien alloy that would destroy it. There were, in fact, some grounds for this contention. Indeed, over a century earlier Judah Halevi had already remarked about a view that some philosophically minded Jews also held in Maimonides' day. In his *Kuzari,* a spokesman for this position is made to say: "Human actions are but instruments which lead up to philosophical heights. Having reached these I care not for religious ceremonies."[13]

But Maimonides' whole approach belied this facile trend. Knowing that the philosopher and the simple person of faith have different motivations and goals, Maimonides' great intellectual effort was to show that the two were not contradictory. For him, in fact, philosophy and (biblical) revelation were complementary paths to God and perfection. To be sure, the former was the rational way of the individual and the latter the faithful way of the community. But since the Jewish philosopher was also enjoined to obey the commandments of the revelation and participate in the halakhic consensus of the community, the role of philosophy could only enhance the participation of the philosopher in Jewish practice. For a long time such arguments fell on deaf ears; and the actual practice of many who pretended to philosophical interests seemed to confirm the ti-rades of the more literal traditionalists. It was a century and more before the steam of controversy evaporated somewhat, and it be-came clear that Maimonides' whole concern was to exalt Torah and the service of God.

The study of Maimonides' *Guide* went into some eclipse until the nineteenth century, when a new wave of rationalism burst on the Jewish scene. Even then, as earlier, this work was not popular among most Jews. For them, the more literalist style of Jewish belief fostered in France and Germany held sway, as did a whole range of mystical interpretations of Scripture and the commandments. In fact, a significant Jewish mystical revival developed in and around thirteenth-century Spain and spread to all the lands of Jewish settle-ment. Not the least of the motivations for this revival was a rejection of philosophical rationalism and allegory. Slowly, a new symbolic language emerged that dominated the nature and imagery of Juda-ism for centuries.

The Mystical Path

The dominant image for the mystical path may be "the maiden in the palace." It is an image made famous by Moses de Leon in his monumental mystical work *Zohar*, or *The Book of Splendor* (thir-teenth century, Spain). Referring to different levels of interpreting Torah and thus approaching God, the text likens the Torah to "a beautiful damsel who is hidden in a secluded room of her palace." She "has a secret lover" who "for love of her . . . keeps passing the gate of her house." And "what does she do? She opens the door of her hidden room ever so slightly and for a moment reveals her face to her lover." This she does gradually, out of love for him; and only he who loves her sees this and is drawn nigh. "So it is with the word of the Torah," says the text, "which reveals herself only to those who love her." The mystic (called the "wise of heart") is thus drawn to God through the Torah and its hints to him. Gradually, out of mu-tual faithfulness, the "hidden secrets" of God's Scripture are revealed to the lover, who, joined in understanding and love to the maiden, is called a "bridegroom of the Torah." Mystical longing is thus consummated with the bliss of understanding.[14]

Faced with the starkness and transcendence of the divine will, many Jews from antiquity on yearned for contact with the living God and for the hidden knowledge derived thereby. Already in early Tannaitic-Amoraic sources a type of Throne Mysticism is indicated, whereby mystical adepts ascended the cosmic spheres to behold in bliss the cosmic Chariot and Throne of God. Here, moreover, in this otherworldly focus one might also be vouchsafed the knowledge of the end of the world. Such a yearning was common in early rabbinic circles and expresses the somewhat world-weary hopes of those subjugated to the dominion of Greece and Rome and downtrodden by the fall of the Temple and the suppression of national hopes. To be sure, this did not lead to any lesser interest in the divine commandments. In fact, some of the great early mystical seekers—like Rabbi Akiba himself—were among the great halakhic specialists. Moreover, these otherworldly speculations did not proceed from outside the Torah, but rather from the reinterpretation of the prophetic and other scriptural passages.

Particular mention should be made in this regard concerning the mystical speculations of the anthropomorphic grandeur and form of God that developed at this time. Such speculations, which derived in part from reinterpreations of passages from the Song of Songs, led in the Middle Ages to a whole anthropormorphic literature about the enormous humanlike features of God—the so-called *Shi'ur Komah* literature. While such speculations were a natural outgrowth of the biblical statement that humans are in the "image of God," they were nevertheless the subject of harsh critiques by the philosophers. These latter felt that such an anthropomorphic focus was a misreading and distortion of scriptural language. Certainly the strong anti-anthropomorphic concerns of Saadia (the Gaon of Sura) and Maimonides were motivated as much by a prophetlike rejection of such "images" of God as by purely philosophical principles. In any case, the ancient Jewish mystics studied and interpreted Scripture with an eye to its deeper spiritual or mystical sense, later called *sod*. This level of meaning was understood to supplement *but not replace* the other levels: of *peshat*, of *derash*, and of *remez*. The *sod* included hidden

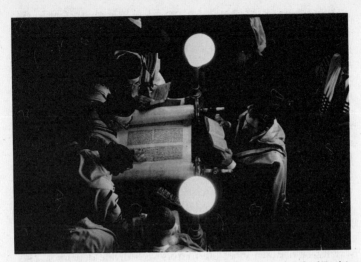

Yom Kippur Torah reading, contemporary Leningrad. Public reading and study of Torah is a sacred duty in Judaism. For Jews it is a renewal of the covenant and testimony to the ever-new teachings of ancient Scripture. Photo credit: Bill Aron.

secrets of God's majestic realm, his form and glory, and the times of the end of history.

The *Zohar* provides one classical expression of the mystical trends current in Judaism in the Middle Ages. As with Maimonides, Moses de Leon also speaks of *sitre torah* ("secrets of Torah"), but these are now given a distinctly mystical (even mythical) meaning. While continuing earlier trends, the *Zohar* reflects a strong reaction to the abstractions and spiritualizations of the philosophers of the day and reconstructs Judaism—through new scriptural interpretations—on a strikingly new foundation. God was no longer perceived as separate from the world, as in the Bible, or utterly abstract and beyond attribution, as in the philosophical literature. God was rather understood as both the transcendent source of all being and the immanent presence of divinity in all things. Thus all creation and creativity was portrayed as flowing out of the infinity of God. Indeed, in the mystical apprehension, God's "image"—his complex structure of attributes (like mercy, power, generativity, and receptivity) and their interrelationships—is to be found in all life and in humans most fully. Thus, as the *Zohar* never ceases to emphasize, what "is below" is mirrored "on high" and vice versa. This being so, God is believed to be inseparable from the life of the world, being its ultimate influence. But, correspondingly, God is also believed to be subject to human influences, through actions and prayer, precisely because humans are so fully "in the image of God."

All these mysteries and more are contained in the Torah when correctly understood through the symbolism of *sod*, for the Torah is not merely a book of narratives and laws. "In the mystery of truth," as the *Zohar* says, the biblical narratives of individual and national history and the laws expressing patterns of proper action are most deeply concerned with the mysterious dynamics in the divine realm, for example, the mysterious relations between mercy and justice or the flow of perfection generated through the unification of such opposites as male and female. The mystical adept is privileged to learn of this deeper truth of the biblical text and, correspondingly, of the way his or her own inner life mirrors such divine dynamics. This knowledge of "higher things" is therefore no mere abstract privilege; its concrete effects are everywhere visible. In the degree to which individual and social life is unified and in harmony, the divine realm (of which human and social life is a part) is correspondingly strengthened; and the degree to which disintegration and discord run rampant in the human realm produces a corresponding fate in the totality of life and being.

For the Jewish mystic, then, the service of God through observance of the commandments is nothing less than a double act of personal and cosmic integration. Indeed, through a life of halakhic performances and prayer the mystic understands and enacts the deepest *sod* (mystery) of being, for he or she is in the privileged position to establish hidden cosmic harmonies *even as* his or her actions establish social order and psychological integration. Thus the this-worldly focus of classical rabbinic Judaism, which saw in Torah study and obedience to the *mitzvot* a means to *tikkum olam* (the rectification of social life), is not bypassed by the mystic. In the performance of the *halakha*, the mystic combines this feature of religious action with the philosopher's and moralist's concern for *tikkun ha-middot* (the rectification of psychological qualities through proper study and observance) in pursuit of the ultimate goal: cosmic *tikkun* (or the rectification and unification of the divine spheres). Indeed, for the mystical path, this otherworldly realm is the true focus of human intention in the faithful observance of the commandments.

Earlier, in connection with Akiba's martyrdom, the medieval adage referring to the unity of Israel and Torah was mentioned. In fact, this adage derives from the ideology of the Zoharic tradition just reviewed. In another formulation of it, the maxim states that "God, Israel, and Torah are one." Now a complete explication of this statement would involve discussing the mystical identities between the three terms in the supernal realms. Nevertheless, some sense of the adage has already been indicated, for since the Torah is an earthly expression of mysterious truths of God and since the commandments of the Torah given to Israel are the true means of establishing divine unity, the three terms comprise one interdependent whole.

Thus, both as an expression of historical reality (the fateful bond between God, Torah, and Israel in the world) and as an expression of theological truth (the mysterious unity between God, Torah, and Israel in the sustenance of this world and all cosmic realms), the foregoing adage captures many layers of Judaism in the Middle Ages. Not the least do we sense here the combination of two of its most salient features: the pathos of Jewish historical destiny and the self-proclaimed privileges of those who believed that their religious life served worldly and otherworldly ends. The gradual penetration of these attitudes into all strata of the Jewish people gave much of medieval Jewish life its distinct character. The belief in the cosmic power of the commandments was also the lever for some powerful eruptions of messianic activity in the sixteenth and seventeenth centuries. Such eruptions and beliefs appear, in retrospect, as among the final expressions of a worldwide Jewish consensus.

Convergences of Paths and Periods

Before turning from medieval to modern Judaism, something should be said of the convergence within historical Jewish life of many of the features just discussed, for it would appear, at first view, that each of the periods just described was utterly separate and that each of the paths and expressions quite distinct. Naturally, classical Judaism is not medieval Judaism, and the philosophical and mystical paths are not one and the same. Still, to not appreciate the organic relations of all these would do considerable disservice to Judaism as it has been lived and continues to be lived.

First, we should simply emphasize the fact that the texts of the classical phase of Judaism continued to be studied in all successive phases, so that the ideologies and halakhic regulations of the early rabbis continued to be discussed and practiced in successive generations. Rabbinical scholars, in fact, constantly related and correlated their various sources and tried to resolve differences between scholarly opinions sometimes spanning more than a thousand years. Their legal and aggadic literature reflects this constant interchange, and the anthological character of so much Jewish medieval literature bears this out as well. There were moral and mystical compendia and aggadic and legal ones. Here many opinions sit alongside one another, all part of one stream of tradition. In many cases, just this anthological character denotes the open-endedness of all discussions. Indeed, already in the Talmud sages over many centuries are found in close anthological proximity. Further, in the prayer book,the Jew could read thrice daily through a literature replete with many levels of tradition: from the biblical psalms to Tannaitic rulings and prayers to medieval hymns and poems. In this form, the full sweep of the tradition is constantly intoned in the community. And finally, the very format of the Rabbinic Bibles (the *Mikra'ot Gedolot*) from the sixteenth century on demonstrate the simultaneity of diverse interpretations in the lifetime of the Jew; every folio page is covered with dozens of commentaries from the first to the nineteenth centuries, with the biblical text in large boldface in the center. The ongoing and often polyvalent voice of tradition was thus an ever-present reality for the Jew (scholar and layperson alike) in both the synagogue and the study house.

It bears further comment in this connection that the creativity of the elite scholars was not compartmentalized, and simultaneous involvement in many levels of writing and thinking was not a rare phenomenon. Thus Akiba was both a halakhic lawyer and a mystic, as was Nachmanides a thousand years later, and Joseph Karo several centuries after him. Similarly, Akiba commented on the Bible and rabbinic literature, as did Rashi and Rashbam and Nachmanides. On the other hand, Saadia was a Bible commentator and a philosopher, as was Rabbi Levi ben Gerson centuries later. Maimonides, as we have seen, not only wrote a vast legal code but composed a rational philosophical treatise as well. Rabbi Joseph Karo, by contrast, not only wrote a legal code and folios of rational legal argument but also commented on the *Mishnah* through the mediation of a heavenly guide, which revealed legal instructions to him after he repeatedly recited portions of this legal text in mantralike fashion (also a practice of other mystics in his circle). Moses de Leon, the reputed author of the *Zohar*, was both a philosopher and mystic (in succession), and his contemporary Abraham Abulafia combined the language and worldview of philosophy (notably of Maimonides' works) with a highly arcane linguistic technique for achieving mystical ecstasy. Quite clearly, some of the most diverse intellectual patterns and interest could be sustained by rabbinic scholars within a fixed, but broadly interpreted, halakhic framework. And as it was for the scholar, so it was for the layperson, though naturally at more modest levels. Indeed, a full grasp of the entire intellectual-religious tradition was an ideal for all. And all were encouraged to roam the rooms of this superstructure, built on the firm base of halakhic conformity.

Perhaps the very anchor of this remarkable diversity was the ancient belief—constantly echoed—that God produces new meanings of Torah every day and that *all* are "the words of the living God." The Torah has at least seventy facets, says a Talmudic tradition; and one medieval mystic even said that it had six hundred thousand—one for every Jew who heard the revelation of Sinai. Thus Torah was always believed to be a religious kaleidoscope of meanings, the rich product of God. To be sure, some meanings had to be fixed for ritual and halakhic life, but many others, of a more aggadic and speculative character, remained more fluid. In all, the diverse meanings of the four traditional methods of interpreting Scripture—*peshat, derash, remez,* and *sod*—were believed to constitute the simultaneous truths of one Torah.

By the Middle Ages, these four levels were coordinated more conceptually and known by the acronym *pardes*. *Pardes* itself means "garden," and this term soon became symbolic of the vest sphere of divine knowledge. As *pardes* was one, so no layer of Scripture cancelled any other. Naturally, the halakhist gave chief emphasis to legal *derash*, while the philosopher and mystic emphasized the levels of *remez* and *sod*. Indeed, the philosopher and mystic commonly believed that these latter levels were of highest significance, and their evaluation of the *peshat* and the purposes of halakhic action were affected by this scale of values. We have indicated some aspects of this in our review of the paths of philosophy and mysticism in medieval Judaism.

The Modern Period (from the eighteenth century to the present)

If we survey the scene of Jews and Judaism from the eighteenth century on from the perspective of our essential matrix of elements, one is struck by both the patterns of continuity and discontinuity. On the one hand, traditional Jewish life continued along quite established channels. As the period opened, the religious authority of the rabbis remained in force, and rabbinic procedure and courts controlled most areas of public and personal law. The halakhic consensus guided the daily and ceremonial life of the Jew in a full manner, and very little was not regulated by it. The Torah and its interpretations dominated the religious imagination and creativity, and this literature was pretty much the only literature traditional Jews read and studied. And the people of Israel remained in the physical and theological state of *galut*, and so felt themselves in exile from their homeland and aliens in the lands of their settlement.

To be sure, all was not static. Corruption in rabbinic leadership in eastern Europe, the lingering crisis of failed messianic expectations, and the effects of violent persecutions were among the factors that lead to the emergence of new Jewish communal patterns and religious structures in southern Poland and the Ukraine in the eighteenth and nineteenth centuries. Particularly significant was the emergence of the pietist movement called Hasidism. In it greater emphasis was placed on personal relations with God and the community than on Torah study and halakhic discourse; and more value was given to the redemptive powers of joy and psychological integration than to ascetic acts of penitence and attempts to influence cosmic harmonies (features of older mystical practice). The new leaders were charismatic teachers and healers called *Tzaddikim*, rather than rabbinic scholars and halakhic experts. In one fell swoop, the pious acts and paradoxical teachings of these holy masters produced a groundswell that renovated the Jewish tradition from within.

Antitraditionalist in some respects (particularly in attitudes toward study, fixed prayer hours, and types of decorum), the new Hasidic movement provoked all the vituperative reactions of a "counterreformation" among the more rational traditionalists, who continued the more intellectual patterns of study and authority. The merest denigration of study was opposed; and the emotional emphases of Hasidic life, together with its belief in the power of the *Tzaddikim* to serve as religious mediators between the people and God, provoked ridicule and censure among those for whom the hallmark of Judaism was emotional propriety and the capacity of each person to stand before God. Yet the threat of a common enemy—outright secularism and radical religious reform—eventually pulled the Hasidim and their opponents (called Mitnaggedim) together. On occasion, the reaction to change was so severe as to provoke attempts to freeze the tradition. Maxims like "change is forbidden from the Torah" from such celebrated halakhists as Rabbi Akiba Eiger reflect the fears of traditionalists. Further symptomatic of these fears were the severe constraints imposed in matters of dress, language, and manner, let alone halakhic innovation. It is therefore not uncommon to see extreme traditionalists to this day dress in the "high style" of nineteenth-century Poland and convinced that "orthodoxy" means inflexibility to change.

Other traditionalists sought to renew the powers of their religious life in other ways: through attempts to renovate the more abstruse patterns of Talmud study that had developed and alienated all but halakhic virtuosi; through attempts to return to more demanding lives of esoteric study and penitential rigor; and through attempts to regenerate religious practice through emphasis on such traditional values as humility, self-scrutiny, and secret service to the poor (the so-called *musar*, or moralist, movement). The renovation of Talmud study led to the founding of great new rabbincal academies, like the celebrated *yeshiva* (rabbinic academy) founded in Volozhin, Lithuania. The return to esoteric piety led to the renewal of Cabalistic study in such celebrated mystical groups as the *"kloiz"* of Brody, Lithuania. And the concern to regenerate flagging or routinized piety through *musar* was the life work of Rabbi Israel Salanter.

But for all the power of these movements and many others that developed from them along more liberal lines the tide of nontradition was rising and threatened to flood Judaism everywhere. It is the discontinuities with tradition that began to emerge in European

Jewish life in the eighteenth and nineteenth centuries that set apart this new period from all those that preceed it. In effect, the continuity of tradition was now just one feature among a great many expressions of Judaism on the historical stage. A clear consensus was a matter to be sought; it could not simply be pointed to.

By the mid-eighteenth century, western and central Europe were undergoing a social and ideological revolution. The class hierarchies of the medieval world were breaking down; notions of the "rights of man" began to develop and spread; ideas of equality among all peoples were advocated and fought for; and a shift in patterns of authority and privilege was in the air. The result was that marginal or suppressed social classes like the Jews were given unprecedented access to education and culture. For virtually the first time Jews mixed with Gentiles on a common basis and had access to new professions. Common political ideals were formed, and Jews became increasingly devoted to the civil laws and educational curricula of the nations in which they lived. All this pulled them farther and farther away from an exclusive reliance on Jewish tradition and put greater demands on this tradition to conform to the new realities.

The social transformations of Jewish life were accompanied by profound shifts of ideology and value. The new "open" cultural climate of Europe—itself a revolutionary rejection of medieval patterns—advocated the ideals of reason and intellectual daring (one motto of this period, the Enlightenment, was Lat. *aude sapere*, "dare to know"). No longer was there a traditional, pregiven and predetermined social-religious reality that people incorporated in themselves with mother's milk, as it were. Now the extent and nature of one's Jewish practice and identity would have to be chosen over against other religious and cultural options available in the society-at-large. This now meant that, for all practical purposes, one's Jewish identity was a matter of personal choice, not just fate. Naturally many Jews experienced intense conflict as they tried to balance new thoughts with traditional ones. One famous example of a search for an intellectual-religious synthesis based on these new realities was that of Moses Mendelssohn (1729–86). In his celebrated volume *Jerusalem*, Mendelssohn formulated a Jewish ideology for the Age of Reason, a Judaism that conforms to natural reason in all its social-moral teachings and that is distinct only in its revealed ceremonial laws. The acceptance of this philosopher into Berlin intellectual society became a celebrated example for liberal Jews and non-Jews alike. It suggested that, with the appropriate adjustment of traditional education and habits, the Jew could "make it" in gentile society. It was not a message that all Jews wanted to hear. Still, new attempts to integrate Judaism with general culture followed; and these paved the way for religious reforms on an unprecedented scale (see Chapter IV).

All told, these changes were momentous and had an profound effect on the status of Torah and tradition. Earlier, when new values and concerns emerged from within the community or from without, they were set against tradition for evaluation. Now the situation was paradoxically reversed; now it was tradition that was set against the nontraditional values for evaluation. The result was that the ancient texts and rituals of Judaism were reevaluated. The Torah was now viewed as a changing and historically conditioned document (in accordance with new historical ideas), and the moral and legal content was judged accordingly. Judaism as a system of thought and practice was now seen in historically relative terms—not as some absolute and timeless essence. In response, some Jews rejected Judaism entirely as a pre-Enlightenment stage of religious culture. Others were spurred to rethink and reform the old faith, for if Judaism was no timeless essence but the ongoing historical product of Jewish creativity, the fate of the religion was something humans could and should take responsibility for. And this many did. A deep alliance therefore developed between those who studied Jewish sources "scientifically" (the movement was called "The Scientific Study of Judaism") and those who wished to present Judaism as an evolving religious-cultural civilization. If (to allude to our opening Talmudic legend) the pressures of modernity forced traditionalists increasingly to emphasize the "Torah of Moses revealed by God," the spirit of modernity also encouraged many others to stress the ever-changing human "interpretations of Akiba and the rabbis." The new ideal was to take historical responsibility for Judaism and Jewish culture and thus through moderate or radical reform to bring traditional Jewish values and practices "into the modern world."

Perhaps the most unexpected cultural reform, and equally the most revolutionary, was the attempt beginning in the late nineteenth century to revive the Jewish nation in its ancestral homeland. This reformist-nationalist movement is known as **Zionism**. Faced with a growing resurgence of anti-Semitism throughout Europe and Russia, many Jews came to fear that civic acceptance by non-Jews was not to be trusted and that they alone had to provide the means for their physical and cultural preservation. Old canards of the gentiles that the Jews were a "state within the state" and subject to "dual loyalties" provoked old Jewish reactions and convinced them that despite apparent social advances they were still "a nation that dwells apart." Under the leadership of Theodor Herzl and others a concern to reform Jewish national life by establishing a new national settlement in Palestine was generated. A major plank in this platform was thus to ensure the physical safety and enfranchisement of Jews, when they could not rely upon their host country. The rescue of Jews from the bloodbath of Nazism after 1945 and of oriental Jews from Arab persecutions after the national State of Israel was founded in 1948 proved to all the essential importance of political Zionism. The role of Israel in providing a safe haven for oppressed Russian, Iranian, and Ethiopian Jews in the 1970s and 1980s has reinforced this attitude.

Thus, after almost two thousand years of exile, the Jews began to restore their ancestral nation and homeland, to revive the ancient Hebrew language, and to rebuild their political and cultural institutions. Indeed, after nearly two millennia of being powerless resident aliens, outside history and national states, many Jews sought to return to history and the task of building a society on a new Jewish basis. This spiritual-cultural aspect of Zionism is its second plank and was considered central to Zionist ideology by some of its earliest leaders, like Ahad Ha-Am. Rejecting many of the attitudes and patterns of traditional Judaism, the new cultural Zionists sought to establish a vigorous nontraditional Jewish culture *on the foundations* of its ancient heritage. This powerful reaction to tradition, together with its strong tone of self-reliance, alienated many traditional Jews from Zionism in the early years, for these traditionalists would not relinquish the ancient image of Zion as a religious symbol of Jewish historical fulfillment and the "return of Zion" as a messianic event to be inaugurated by God alone. Other, more temperate attitudes developed within traditional circles, and forms of religious Zionism gradually emerged in central Europe and America. Today, religious Zionism is a vital component in the reshaping of Jewish life in Israel providing a strong share of new immigrants and challenging secular or non-Jewish law and values with the teachings of tradition. Attempts to form a viable synthesis between traditional *halakha* and custom and Western liberal humanism and its values are a major feature of the legal-cultural agenda of the modern State of Israel—though not without intense vigilance and lobbying on both sides to ensure that their "interests" are safeguarded and enhanced.

The development and revival of Jewish cultural in Israel has had an incalculable effect on the nature of Jewish life elsewhere, particularly in twentieth-century America. It has generated new national pride, stimulated study of Hebrew and Jewish literature, and restored Israel to a land of pilgrimage for all. As the first cultural Zionists hoped, Israel has proved to be a center and catalyst for Jewish creativity everywhere. In addition, as a result of Zionism, new bonds have been formed between Jews the world over, so that the ancient value that "all Jews are responsible for each other" has received new meaning in the second half of the twentieth century. Massive financial and emotional support has been tendered the fledgling state by North American Jews especially; and Russian and other recent immigrants to Israel have been sustained by world Jewish charities. All this is done with the ancient virtue of self-help and with a new nonapologetic pride in Jewish destiny. For these reasons, Jews growing up after 1948 hardly conceive of a time when the Jewish people were harassed and utterly powerless. This has led to a revision of historical memory in some cases. Nevertheless, the constant concern to memorialize the murder of six million Jews during World War II keeps the pain of the Jewish historical past alive and has motivated a vigilant attitude that "never again" will Jews be powerless and unprepared in the face of persecution. Such collective attitudes have served to reinforce the sense among modern Jews that they remain one people, however scattered they may be across the globe and however diverse they may be with respect to their religious practices. In fact, this powerful concern for the preservation of the Jewish people serves virtually as the new consensus of Jewish life, binding traditional and nontraditional Jews to a common purpose.

Another virtual consensus of modern Judaism, despite all the variations and reinterpretations to which it has been subject, including the secular revision of its ancient symbols and terms, is the ancient calendar cycle. Whether they are traditionalists, nontraditionalists, or post-traditionalists and whether they are fundamentalists, liberals, or secularists, all modern Jews who are in any way conscious of their religious-national heritage acknowledge the Jewish New Year and the ancient national festivals in some way, for to live utterly and deliberately outside the traditional Jewish units of time—no matter how much these may be, for some, secondary to the civil calendar—is to live utterly and deliberately outside any expression of Jewish life. Thus today as much as in earlier times the calendar cycle carries the forms of Jewish life and sensibility. It is to the traditional pattern of this cycle that we now turn. Indeed, in one form or another these patterns still mark the physiognomy of modern Judaism.

■

CHAPTER III

Judaism as a Ritual System

I n traditional Judaism, all aspects of life are ritualized through halakhic regulations—from the first thoughts and prayers in the morning through the final prayers upon one's bed at night, from permitted and unpermitted foods to permitted and unpermitted business practices, from the obligations of daily prayer to the requirements of festival celebration and personal mourning. Accordingly, all aspects of life take on the legal character of *mutar* and *asur*, or "permitted" and "forbidden," acts; and such other categories as *hayyav* and *patur*, or "obliged" and "free" (not obliged), and *qodesh* and *hol*, or "holy" and "profane" also dominate the daily religious consciousness and experience of the traditional Jew. Accordingly, the observant Jew will be typically scrupulous in performing his or her halakhic obligations, that is, highly attentive to the proper times and manner of performing the commandments. And further, since this pattern of performance is not merely individual, but often depends upon a quorum of others, halakhic observance also brings the Jew into conformity with other members of the community who feel equally "bound" by the legal-religious strictures of the *halakha*.

Invariably, then, the personal and interpersonal pattern of halakhic life dramatizes the ideology of Judaism in concrete forms. And it is just these forms that give the beliefs and attitudes of Judaism their daily texture, their lived quality. It has therefore been observed that the calendar is the true Jewish theology or ideology, for it is the calendar and its content that carries Judaism from one moment to the next. Indeed, the beliefs of Judaism become present each day through the prayers, study, and life actions of the Jew, for each act (ideally) brings to mind the historical memories, ritual affirmations, and moral values upon which Judaism is based. There is thus no abstract affirmation of faith in Judaism. Rather, one performs the *halakha* and, through it, affirms Jewish values and ideals. Characteristically, a traditional Jew is not called a "believer" but a *shomer mitzvot*, an "observer of the commandments," and a traditional Jew is not considered pious in the abstract but only through being quit of the halakhic obligation required on a given occasion. Halakhic piety is thus an ongoing expression—daily and seasonal—of Jewish religious life.

Before turning to the rituals themselves, a brief word about the all-important calendar is in order. First, the present calendar of traditional Judaism is lunisolar; that is, the months are reckoned according to the phases of the moon and the years according to the circuit of the sun. Now since a solar year exceeds a lunar one (12 months) by about 11 days and since, too, the festivals are fixed both by the moon and by agricultural seasons, which are dependent upon a tropical solar year, the cycle of lunar months must be adjusted. If this were not done, the festivals would "wander" backwards, and the spring festival of Passover would eventually come in the winter and then in the summer. At the present time, the adjustment means the addition of an extra month (Adar II) 7 times in 19 years. For daily ritual purposes, time reckoning is deemed to begin at the end of twilight (i.e., after sunset, with the rising of the moon). Special rituals occur in connection with the new moon each month; and the beginning of a new lunisolar cycle is celebrated by holy convocations, as we shall see.

It may be noted that, from biblical antiquity through the Middle Ages, the proper determination of the calendar was a major preoccupation and a source of bitter controversy. Many factors entered into these disputes, including (among the Qumran sectarians and others) belief in a purely solar reckoning. Of particular significance was the concern for a ritual or halakhic consensus among all Jews—based, naturally, on what each group believed to be the true interpretation of the biblical cycle of holy seasons. Dramatic breaks within ancient and medieval Judaism and of course between early Judaism and Christianity thus found concrete expression in calendrical terms. For example, when the early church determined that the Sabbath was to be reckoned on Sunday and not on Saturday (as was the custom from ancient biblical times) or that Easter could not fall on the Passover festival, it became effectively impossible for early Christians (committed to Jesus as Messiah) to also remain Jews in practice. Similarly, the reckoning of time relative to the life of Jesus (e.g., A.D.) and the adjustment of the months to the pagan Roman civil calendar further distinguished the two communities. For Jews time was reckoned, through biblical chronologies, back to the creation, and the beginning of the year coincided with a late Babylonian calendar (discussed below). Thus the Jewish new year beginning in autumn 1986 (4–5 October of that year, but varying slightly in other years) was celebrated by Jews worldwide as the year 5477 since the creation of the world. Some Jews have also dated their times from the fall of the Temple in 70 C.E., but this was never common practice. Thus, even by such broad computational matters, the calendar conveys the significant religious and historical orientations of those who live by its structures.

The Calendrical Cycle of Holiness

Daily Prayers and Patterns

The cycle of holiness begins for the traditional Jew upon awakening. The *halakha* regulates these initial acts, as it does all others. At this time it is customary (for the male after putting on a skullcap, called *kipa* or *yarmulke*) to wash and recite prayers that reflect the dependence of the human creature on the creator and the need to be respectful of this attitude at all times. One of these morning prayers, and often the first young children are taught, states: "I give thanks to You, living and enduring King, who has restored me to my soul, with the great grace of Your trustworthiness. The beginning of wisdom is the fear of the Lord. . . . [whose] praise is everlasting." A series of prayers that emphasize the divine gift of knowledge, of daily sustenance and care, and of the consciousness of Jewish identity and its obligations begins the order of the service. These may be recited alone or with the community at morning worship. Traditionally, this prayer service and all other obligations whose "time is fixed" (a halakhic category) are incumbent upon the male but not obligatory for women with household responsibilities. Some of women's fixed obligations will be mentioned later.

All males thirteen years and over are required to pray three times daily, and to wear phylacteries during the morning service. These phylacteries, called *tefillin*, are ritual prayer boxes containing biblical quotations that are secured to the forehead and customarily left arm by leather straps. This ancient practice is based on the biblical passages that say that one should bind the teachings of God as a "sign upon your hand and frontlets between your eyes," that is, as a constant reminder of divine duties. The *tefillin* on the head now symbolizes the obligation to serve God with one's mind and the one on the arm, near the heart, symbolizes divine service with one's emotions. In early rabbinic times and through the Middle Ages especially, saintly persons wore *tefillin* at all times. Women are also permitted to wear them, but have been customarily discouraged from this practice until very recent times and only among certain more liberal though traditionally minded Jews. Similarly, a male wears a prayer shawl, called **tallit**, with special knots and fringes during daily morning prayers, though the prayer leader also wears it at afternoon and evening services. It is common for Jews to raise the shawl over their heads in prayer as a means of facilitating private devotion and concentration. Very traditional males also wear such fringes attached to a type of undergarment, thus further fulfilling an ancient biblical injunction. Such prayer garments are not customary for women, though the outer shawl has begun to be worn in recent years. The purpose of the fringes is to aid one "to remember all [the] commandments."

The opening section of the morning prayers are comprised of biblical psalms, and of rabbinic prayers especially emphasizing the themes of creation, revelation, and redemption. Thus a variety of historical and theological issues are brought to mind, particularly one's dependence upon God in nature and history and the obligations one owes God for his guidance and teachings. The affirmation of divine unity (the Shema prayer, cited earlier) is a major event in this part of the service (and again when recited in the evening service). For Jews it is a moment of personal and collective testimony to the principles of monotheism—the unity of God and all life under God. So central is this affirmation that it is customarily recited before sleep and as part of the death confession. It was also recited by Jews who died a martyr's death on account of these very principles.

A major prayer—called, in fact, "The Prayer" (*ha-Tefilla*)—climaxes the morning, and virtually every Jewish service. The morning version has traditionally eighteen separate prayers (fewer on the Sabbath). These prayers proceed from praise to petition (for wisdom and health, for justice and peace, and for the restoration of the kingship of David and the ancient Temple service). "The Prayer" is silently recited while standing—hence it is also called "The Standing Prayer" or *Amida*—and immediately repeated aloud by the prayer leader along with a series of sanctifications recited communally. On Mondays and Thursdays (ancient market days), the weekly Torah portion is read publicly in an abbreviated form, so that all Jews might "fulfill the commandment" of Torah study in public. Final prayers concerned with personal needs and collective redemption conclude the service.

The afternoon (*minhah*) and evening (*ma'ariv*) service are more abbreviated versions of the morning (*shaharit*) worship, with occasional variations on it. Most significantly, the Shema is recited twice daily, and "The Prayer" and an Adoration are recited in all three daily services. The Adoration is recited with great reverence (and in ancient and medieval times and still today on special occasions with an act of genuflection). It opens with the words: "It is incumbent upon us to praise the Master of All . . . who has not dealt with us as with other peoples." Acknowledging their special historical destiny, Jews go on to recite the messianic hope. "We therefore hope in You . . . to speedily see the splendor of Your might"—the end of idolatry, the national restoration of Jews to their homeland, and the reunification of all the peoples of the earth. The concluding line of the Adoration is commonly sung by all as the great climax of worship: "And as it has been said (in Scripture): the Lord will be king over all the earth; on that day the Lord will be One, and His Name One."

Only after morning prayers does the traditional Jew eat breakfast. All meals are preceded by a ritual handwashing (with prayer) and a benediction over the food: "Blessed are You, Lord our God, king of the universe, who brings forth bread from the earth". Other blessings for other foods can be substituted, and these are carefully fixed by rabbinic *halakha*. After the meal, a cycle of prayers in thanks to God "who sustains all life" is recited. And all through the day, special events in nature (like seeing marvels or the simple wonder of a sunset) or between persons (like reunions and partings or beholding human grandeur or despair) can be the occasion for special prayers. In all this there is to be found a religious attentiveness to all life as a divine gift. An old rabbinic dictum states that one who receives the benefits of the earth without thanking God is "like a thief."

We may recall here the statement of Maimonides cited earlier, that the goal of the commandments is to teach the Jew proper service of God in all things. We may add, given that Maimonides was the author of a legal code, that this service extended from the prayer house to the community and business world. From the traditional perspective, the performance of all one's behaviors within the moral framework established by halakhic regulations (recall the categories of the *Mishnah*) was also a form of acknowledgement of divine lordship. There is thus daily verbal prayer (petition and praise) and daily nonverbal action (halakhic duty). Each in its own way expresses subservience to divine rule. Not restricting themselves to fixed halakhic regulations, the pietists called Hasidim further devoted themselves to serve God in all ways at all times. They spoke of *avoda be-gashmi'ut*, "service through physical nature," by which they meant the concern to sanctify God's creation in every way, even through the most mundane physical acts. By this they only expressed in a more passionate way the basic religious assumption of halakhic Judaism: that service to God is to be performed in and through the concrete details of daily life.

The traditional Jew is thus fully conscious at every moment of every day that he or she is responsible to the Torah and the commandments. Years of training, study, and practice make one highly sensitive to whether actions are halakhically permitted or not—and this sensitivity is, in fact, at a high level of daily awareness. But this does not mean that the traditional Jew normally feels constrained by this orientation or burdened by it, for the immediate goal is to become competent in the traditional practices in order to serve God through the commandments. The greater the skill and competence, the more completely will the practices be internalized and performed with an unconstrained sense of personal inflection. Accordingly, for the traditional Jew the *halakha* is experienced as a divine gift that guides one through the maze of possible actions. Indeed, via the *halakha* a Jew commonly feels the "rightness" and "order" of earthly actions, their "world-building" and "covenant-confirming" character.

Nor do traditional Jews normally feel burdened by the commandments, for their whole goal is obedience to God, and the commandments are the concrete means toward that end. There is thus very great emphasis in Jewish practice on resisting routinized performance and practicing the commandments with attention and joy. In fact, one of the most important value categories related to traditional observance is called *simhah shel mitzvah*, "the joy of the commandment." It may take various forms at various times. One form is mostly affective in nature and leads one to enact the details of the law with visible joy. The Psalmist's dictum to "serve the Lord with gladness" is thus internalized in this mode and given external expression through passionate involvement in the *mitzvot*. The second form of "joy," quite related to the preceding one, is focused on what is called *hiddur mitzvah*, "enhancing the commandment" through additional acts. It is thus the biblical dictum "this is my Lord and I shall exalt Him" that is internalized in this mode and expressed through the constant desire to dramatize one's loving performance of the *mitzvot* by adding more and more features to them. The frequent comment that one has the *mitzvah*, or special merit and opportunity, to perform a given *mitzvah* thus conveys the conviction of the Jew that in and through the joyful performance of the commandments one can continuously express the willing acceptance of God's covenant.

Weekly Prayers and Patterns

Perhaps no occasion in the life of the Jew is more dominated by the obligations of unstinting joy or more focused on the halakhic details of "permitted/forbidden" and "sacred/profane" acts than the Sabbath. Coming each week at Friday dusk and celebrated until Saturday eve (though routinely one "delays concluding the Sabbath and hastens to begin it"—this being *hiddur mitzvah*), the Sabbath is both the climax and focus of the week. Special foods are customarily prepared or set aside for the Sabbath, special guests or unexpected travellers are invited, and the labors and distractions of the work week are consciously disregarded. From classical times to the present day the Sabbath has been the day when every male Jew was king and his wife a queen, when the Jewish nation royally accepted "Queen Sabbath" into its midst, and when the joys of paradise and redemption were anticipated. Already in ancient sources the Sabbath is referred to as a "mystery" of God's, as a special expression of divine grace for the people of Israel. In one old midrashic source it is stated: "If one keeps one Sabbath as it should be kept, the Messiah will come. The Sabbath is equal to all the other precepts of the Torah." In the mystical tradition, the "mystery" of the Sabbath is profounder yet, symbolic of ultimate divine harmonies and cosmic restoration. A passage from the *Zohar* called *raza de-Shabbos*, "the mystery of the Sabbath," is still sung on Friday evening in many synagogues as part of the First Sabbath service.

In a traditional home, the approach of sundown on Friday marks the final stage of Sabbath preparations. Because the Sabbath day traditionally recalls the completion of the creation and God's rest from this labor, no work is permitted on this day. All cooking is completed before the onset of the Sabbath, and perhaps the stove is also lit for reheating the previously cooked food. Electric lights will

Sabbath candlelighting in the eastern European manner (turn of century America, ca. 1901). Lighting candles is a special duty of Jewish women, and the moment is filled with a holy aura and special inwardness of reflection. Photo courtesy of American Jewish Historical Society.

also be switched on in advance of the Sabbath, since the strictly observant consider even the use of noncombustive types of burning produced by electricity an extension of the biblical prohibition against igniting a fire on this day. For this reason, nowadays electrical appliances are also avoided (except the refrigerator, since the surge of current is considered incidental and not the result of intent). In addition, business instruments and money are set aside for the duration of the Sabbath.

When these matters are completed, the more spiritual preparations are undertaken. In certain circles it remains customary to precede the Sabbath with a ritual ablution, to prepare special clothes for use (often white ones, an old symbol for purity and grace), and to get oneself into the proper frame of mind though mental reflection or study of a pious text. It remains customary to recite the Song of Songs, whose contents from ancient rabbinic times have been interpreted allegorically as God's love for Israel. More mystical understandings regard this relationship as symbolic of profound unifications in the divine realms. In many communities, the recitation is done in the synagogue immediately before the inaugural service on Friday (before sunset), when the "Queen Sabbath" is welcomed.

Shortly before sunset two Sabbath candles are lit and blessed by the mother of the home; this is one of her traditional obligations, along with the baking of Sabbath loaves (called *halah*) which are braided in a customary way. The candles and two loaves of bread (for the evening and next day) along with the wine for sanctifying the Sabbath day dominate the table. These accoutrements symbolize the fullness of blessing and resemble the setting of the candelabra and shewbread in the ancient Temple. In fact, an old rabbinic dictum states that "[one's] table is like an altar," and this interpretation gives a heightened ritual aura to the setting.

The traditional Sabbath service begins late Friday afternoon with psalms about the divine Majesty and Kingship, along with a medieval hymn welcoming the Sabbath bride. The regular evening service then continues with some special additions marking the Sabbath day. After these prayers, and throughout the Sabbath, the customary salutation is a blessing for Sabbath peace—in Hebrew *Shabbat Shalom* and in the colloquial Yiddish *gut Shabbos*. After the Sabbath evening service (recited in the synagogue or at home), the family then gathers at table where a special hymn to the "angels of peace" is recited and the children are individually blessed by their parents. Before the adult male recites the benediction over the wine and the sanctification over the day (the Kiddush prayer), he customarily sings a biblical hymn of praise to his wife (Prov. 31:10–31). In mystical understandings, this hymn is directed to the mysteries of cosmic union, symbolized by masculine and feminine imagery. After a ritual handwashing (as at every meal) and a benediction over the bread, a festive meal with traditional songs is enjoyed. If guests are present, they will be invited to lead a song or teach the gathering some "word of Torah." The guest is also often honored with leading the grace after meals.

The special holiness of the Sabbath day is thus marked by a festive mood called *oneg Shabbat*, "Sabbath joy." Indeed, one is enjoined to make the day joyous and different from other days in both deportment and attitude. Certainly the strict restriction ensuring "rest" gives the day a tone and rhythm affected by natural light and natural human relations—not artificial lights or goal-oriented behaviors. Many Jews are also concerned that the topics of conversation befit the spiritual character of the day and that thoughts be restricted to themes of Torah, God, and loving-kindness. Since ancient rabbinic times, in fact, a quasi-legal category called *shevut* has been recommended. This category emphasizes a concern for mental and emotional rest, for a general "letting go" of everyday concerns on the Sabbath.

The full rhythm of the day dramatizes the themes and ideology of Judaism. The Kiddush on Friday eve along with the synagogue hymns stresses the imagery of creation and new beginnings. The morning service on Saturday, which generally expands upon the regular daily service, climaxes with a communal reading of a lesson from the Torah (and also the Prophets), and so celebrates the divine revelation to the nation. And the late afternoon service on Saturday and the concluding prayers "separating" the Sabbath from the week (called the Havadalah, or "Separation" service) give special emphasis to the theme of messianic renewal and redemption. The celebrated medieval author Rabbi Isaac Arama, in his *Akedat Yitzhaq*, stressed that these major phases of the day symbolize the three central themes of Judaism: creation, revelation, and redemption. Moreover, already in ancient times the three phases of the day coincided with three Sabbath meals. In medieval mystical circles, special cosmic significance was attributed to the celebration of each one. More recently, among the Hasidim, the third meal (called *se'udah shelishit*, or colloquially *shale-shudes*) was deemed a most "favorable time" to commune with God, and the rabbi then delivered a special Torah teaching. Rhythmic chants, holy tales, and shared food add to the "messianic" atmosphere of the occasion. An additional fourth meal has been added by some, to prolong the holiness of the day and accompany the Sabbath Queen as she departs from the community. This festive time is called the *melave malke*.

As these final meals are dominated by Torah study, so is the whole Sabbath day affected by it—especially the central ceremony on Saturday morning when the weekly Torah portion is read out loud. It is a momentous occasion, preceded by taking the Torah scrolls from the ark (the Torah is still written on special skins in the ancient script) and parading them around the congregation. All congregants face the processional of the long scrolls, which are robed in fine cloth and adorned with high silver crowns. Many reach out to touch or kiss the holy objects with great veneration. Laid upon a high reading desk, the Torah of Moses is then unfurled and a selection chanted in the ancient melody. This is done each week of the year (with special readings on or near festivals). In ancient times, in the land of Israel, the entire Pentateuch was recited over a three-year period, but the Babylonian custom to conclude the reading in one year now prevails. In more recent times, attempts to abridge the weekly lection have been innovated, but the idea of a continuous and unbroken reading of the Torah remains among traditional Jews. Symbolic of this is the custom of reading a brief excerpt from the following week's portion during the Sabbath afternoon service.

In all these ways the centrality of the Torah in the life of the people is dramatized. Significantly, too, only the Torah lection is read out in the service—even though members of the congregation will follow along with texts that include rabbinic comments, and even though all know that it is just these comments and interpretations that give the Torah its distinctly "Jewish" character. The reason for this is to emphasize the divine word alone and to distinguish that from the history of its interpretation. For the community, this high ceremony of reading the Torah is experienced as a renewal of the ancient revelation. It is therefore an occasion of deep mythic significance for Jews.

Yearly Festivals and Sacred Days

Although some of the festivals are agricultural in origin and others are not, there is calendrical continuity in the fact that the lunar phases that help to reckon the ancient seasons still determine the monthly countings. Thus many festivals occur on the fifteenth day, or full moon, of a month. And there is also a basic symmetry to the calendrical year. For example, preparation for the spring holiday of Passover (Pesah, often in April) begins on the tenth day of the first month (Nisan), and the festival itself commences on the fifteenth and lasts a week. Actually, according to Pharisaic tradition, the first day is celebrated for two days, as is the seventh, hence for a total of eight days, exceeding the biblical requirement. The reason has to do with the ancient problem of notifying communities in the Diaspora, those dispersed throughout other lands, when a new moon preceding a festival was sighted. Owing to communication delays, these communities did not always know if a certain month had thirty days rather than twenty-nine, and so they celebrated the ensuing festival with an extra day at the onset and at the conclusion for precautionary reasons. (This practice has become customary to this day outside the land of Israel, except for Reform Jews). Beginning with the second day of Passover (according to Pharisaic tradition) a period of forty-nine days are counted off, culminating with the festival of Pentecost, or Shavu'ot (celebrated for two days).

Balancing these spring holidays in the first month are a series of autumnal celebrations a half year later. The first of these is the New Year festival, called Rosh Hashanah (observed for two days) at the beginning of the seventh month (Tishri). It is followed ten days later by the Day of Atonement, known as Yom Kippur (a one-day fast). On the fifteenth of the month, the festival of Tabernacles, or Sukkot, is celebrated for a week plus a final eighth day of Solemn Assembly. Because of the custom of adding an extra day, the total holiday period is nine days in all—though since the Middle Ages this last day has been celebrated as a separate holiday called Simhat Torah, the day of the "Rejoicing of the Law." On this day, the annual

Torah reading is both concluded and immediately inaugurated once again. Other annual festivals include the ancient Arbor Day celebration (called Tu Be-Shevat) on the fifteenth of the eleventh month (Shevat), once called the "New Year for Trees," and Purim, celebrating the Jews' ancient deliverance from a threatened persecution in the days of the "Persians and Medes," on the fourteenth of the twelfth (Adar) month (but on the fifteenth day in ancient walled cities, like Jerusalem). The anomaly that the months are counted from the spring but the New Year occurs in the seventh month is due to the adoption during the Babylonian exile of a late Babylonian calendar (and its names).

As mentioned, many of the festivals originally had an agricultural origin (Passover celebrates the ripening of the barley grain; Pentecost is the time of the harvest of first fruits of the soil; and Tabernacles celebrates the ingathering of crops) and served in biblical and rabbinic times as pilgrimage seasons and times of ritual donations to the shrine and Temple. However, from early biblical times, many of these seasonal festivals were given historical significance. Thus the festival of Passover was reinterpreted in biblical antiquity as a commemoration of the Exodus from Egypt; and Pentecost, in later rabbinic times, came to commemorate the revelation of the Torah at Mount Sinai. Similarly, the rabbinically ordained festival of Hanukkah, commencing on the twenty-fifth of the ninth month (Kislev), may originally have been related to solar rites at the winter solstice (the holiday had the ancient name of "Festival of Lights") but came to commemorate the rededication of the Temple and the rekindling in it of the holy flame from pure oil preserved despite the desecration of sacred objects by the Greeks. According to a tradition, this cruze of oil miraculously burned for eight days, so the holiday is celebrated for this many nights with burning candles or wicks.

Other days, like the fast Tisha B'Av on the ninth of the fifth month (Av), may also have had agricultural roots (like the ancient festivals on the fifteenth of that month) but came to commemorate the destructions of the First and Second Temples, as well as the exile from Spain (in 1492). In recent years, this fast day is also a time when the horror of the Holocaust is recalled, though this latter event now also has its own memorial day (on the twenty-seventh of Nisan), immediately prior to the day recalling acts of Jewish heroism and resistance during World War II (on the anniversary of the Warsaw Ghetto uprising). Like these more recent occasions, the ancient and medieval calendar was full of days of fasting and commemoration, though not all are still observed. Thus there are minor fast days (like that commemorating the assassination of the governor Gedalia in biblical times; or the twentieth of the third month [Sivan], which was a major day throughout the Middle Ages for recalling martyrologies), as well as festivals of national liberation (like the day of Nicanor in antiquity; the many Second Purims of the Middle Ages celebrating local victories or release from tyranny; or the Day of Independence in recent times, on the fifth of the second month [Iyyar], celebrating the establishment of the State of Israel in 1948). Like the older festivals and now the newer ones, lore, customs, rituals, special foods, and symbolic interpretations provide the concrete expressions and thoughts of living Judaism.

Quite apart from the historical reinterpretation of the nature festivals of antiquity, another layer—of spiritual interpretation—is commonly added to the symbols and rites of the holidays. This transforms them into days of holiness and contrition, in accordance with the Jewish spirit. Thus, for example, the command to eat unleavened bread (called *matzah*) throughout the Passover period has come to indicate the need for penitential abandonment of the sin of pride and self-aggrandizement (the act of "swelling" with pride or "puffing" oneself up), as symbolized by the forbidden leavened bread. Similarly, the halakhic injunction to search one's home diligently to remove all leavened goods before the holiday has often been interpreted as the need simultaneously to cleanse one's inner being before the festival. In this way the celebration of the historical release from bondage is correlated with an act of personal transformation as well.

But all these and other spiritual reinterpretations of ancient holidays pale in emphasis and depth before the most holy and spiritual of days in the Jewish year: the days that occur before, during, and after the New Year (at the beginning of the seventh month Tishri). This period, known as the Days of Awe, traditionally begins in the preceding month of Elul and extends through the seventh day of Tabernacles (called Hoshana Rabba). It is a time of somber self-scrutiny and acts of repentance. Throughout this time blasts of the ram's horns (*shofar*) are blown, symbolizing the need to awaken from spiritual slumber and return to God. This concern for spiritual and moral renewal (called *teshuvah*) is especially marked during the period from Rosh Hashanah to Yom Kippur, which is known as the "Ten Days of Repentance." On Rosh Hashanah itself all Jews gather for communal prayers and high celebration of Beginnings. The extended synagogue liturgy emphasizes the themes of world and individual renewal; of God as Creator, King, and Judge; of the need for divine mercy; and the humbleness of mortal existence. The services are marked by special liturgical poetry that repeats in many modulations the religious themes of this holy period. Special liturgical melodies, which express the majesty of the divine kingship and the humble neediness of human life, also give the services a special and memorable timbre for the worshipers. The Torah readings chosen for this time and the complementary selections from the Prophets reinforce the liturgical themes as they stress the frailty of ongoing life and the eternal hopes of the human community.

In this connection, it is important to add that links between family and friends are especially marked during this period. Festive meals for relations and others are very much part of the socially integrating customs of the New Year. It is furthermore customary for Jews to visit the graves of ancestors during the period of penitence. In this way earlier generations have beseeched their "righteous dead" to intercede for them and their sins before the Mercy Seat of God and have integrated memories of loss with personal and communal hopes. Jews commonly greet one another during this period with the blessing "May you be written and sealed [in the divine Book of Life] for a good year" and with hopes for "a good and sweet year." On Rosh Hashanah it is traditional to dip apples in honey and to pray for a year of sweet renewal. It is also an old custom among Jews to buy new clothes for the New Year. In this way the prevalent themes of newness are dramatically expressed, for clothes typically symbolize spiritual status and hope. Similarly, many adult males wear white outer garments at this time to symbolize the desire for purity and spiritual rebirth. Often a male will receive and first wear a white robe (colloquially called a *kittel*, after the Greek *kiton*) on his marriage day; he then wears it yearly at the Passover meal, on Yom Kippur, called the "Sabbath of Sabbaths," and finally as a shroud.

Yom Kippur is the climax of the extended period of penitence and renewal beginning in the month of Elul and is observed through strict fasting and self-scrutiny. The liturgy for this most holy day begins a little before sunset (of the tenth of Tishri) and, after a night pause, continues from early the next morning through sunset of that day. This great Day of Awe emphasizes self-examination, repentance, and need for God-centeredness. The liturgy is filled with the hope and confidence of divine mercy, but humbly so; and it is replete with extensive confessions and meditations (read silently and aloud with the community). Significantly, an old ruling in the Mishnah emphasizes that the prayers and ritual of Yom Kippur only atone for sins between the individual and God, not for sins between one person and another. For this reason it is customary to seek personal forgiveness or reconciliation from members of one's family and community before the beginning of the prayers. The Jew thus moves first to strengthen links of interpersonal solidarity and then to the matter of the personal relationship with God. It should be emphasized that the transition to privacy before God is neither abrupt nor final. Throughout the liturgy the individual repeatedly recites confession in a collective voice ("we," "us") and bows down or sings with the community. Nevertheless, Yom Kippur is a time of great interiority and private reflections.

This most holy day ends with a final burst of theological confession and joy at the possibility of new beginnings and the sense of divine forgiveness. The Shema is proclaimed, as is the eternal Kingship of God, and the community joins with songs of hope in a speedy redemption. It is at this time that a long, final blast of the *shofar* is sounded (one hundred blasts are blown on Rosh Hashanah). This final blast is thus no longer a piercing or wailing call for self-awakening and contrition but a triumphant blast that follows the communal proclamation that it is one fellowship under One God. The Jew, robed in the solemn garments of death (the *kittel*) and behaving in many ways like a mourner, goes through an inner process of death and rebirth—like the prophet Jonah, whose story of rebellion, repentance, and renewal (with the symbolism of death and rebirth through the episode of the great fish) is recited on this day. Significantly, at the close of the service family and friends gather for a festive meal that symbolizes the social solidarity of the community as each individual is drawn out of solitariness for the shared tasks of the new year.

As a further gesture of the return from the liminal, liturgical zone of Yom Kippur to the world of the community, it is customary on that very night to begin building an arbor booth, or *sukkah*. It is within this temporary structure that meals are taken during the festival of Tabernacles (Sukkot), which follows five days later. The fragility of the booth and its openness to the high heavens and raw nature symbolize for the Jew the fragility of all earthly constructions and the dependence of all creatures on their Creator. The building of the booth and the celebration of an ancient harvest rite with a bouquet of plants and fruits is thus the first act of world-building after the sustained period of penitential withdrawal beginning in Elul. Its repetition each year is part of the deep myth and ritual of Judaism.

While periods like the Days of Awe involve a balance between personal solitariness and communal solidarity, other holidays, like the festival of Passover (Pesah), give more complete expression to communal celebration. This national holiday emphasizes the collective nature of redemption from bondage in Egypt. It is traditionally celebrated as a family meal and recitation (thus preserving the ancient biblical rite), together with special synagogue observances. The Passover meal, or **seder**, is modeled on an old Roman banquet format (complete with the kinds of hors d'oeuvres Romans ate) but is linked to a recitation, called the *Haggadah*, of the wondrous events of the Exodus. The structure of the recitation involves questions and answers, discussions and rabbinic commentaries, and biblical narratives and hymns. Medieval rounds are sung with great gusto at the finale.

The recollection of redemption and divine power are the recurrent themes of the day; and personal and collective identification with Jewish history are the great imperatives. It is incumbent upon each Jew to identify with the story of the Exodus by elaborating on the original event or by discussions that seek to make the ancient event of liberation relevant in each generation. The Passover meal is also the time of somber historical recollection: the *matzah*, or unleavened bread (eaten during the entire festival), as well as the herbs and condiments eaten symbolize the suffering of the ancient Israelites and the mortar for the bricks during their forced labor. But the central meal, which interrupts the *Haggadah* recitation, is also a time of family joy and ingathering. Central to the family ritual on this night is the youngest child, the bearer of the future, who is raised to preeminence as the initiator of the questions that precede the *Haggadah* recitation. The other young children have other, more gamelike, roles to play in the *seder*, which turn the event into one of great mirth.

A more solemn time in the family service occurs after the meal, when the door of the house is opened to invite the prophet Elijah (the traditional harbinger of the Messiah) to partake of the celebration. This invitation with songs of future redemption has been supplemented since the Middle Ages with a curse against those who have killed the Jews over the centuries. And indeed, in Jewish memory Passover has not only been a time of hope but, falling as it does near Easter, a time of fear, for this was the time of frequent church-sponsored persecutions or vilifying blood libels (Jews being falsely accused, in the Middle Ages and up to recent years, of killing Christian children to use their blood for baking *matzah*). Heinrich Heine's famous story of *The Rabbi of Bacharach* strikes familiar dread in the hearts of Jewish readers. In this tale, at the moment when the door was opened for Elijah, it was not this messianic precursor who entered but rampaging Christian mobs. This and other accounts of destruction and bloodshed were told over and over again in Jewish historical chronicles.

But we should also add that the symbolism of liberation of Passover has also inspired great acts of spiritual resistance. Stories of the celebrations of the Passover in the Warsaw Ghetto and the concentration camps during World War II are as awesome for the human daring involved as they are powerful expressions of the Jewish use of myth and ritual for acts of antihistory, for a rejection of the history of brutality and power in favor of a history of spiritual dedication.

In all these forms, Jewish life has dramatized its deepest convictions and memories. Memory and ideology are thus not abstract matters but concretely represented throughout the course of the calendar year. Quite evidently, then, this calendar cycle determines the rhythm of thoughts and feelings of the Jew the year round, pacing and balancing religious moods and awareness and providing the occasions for living the religion. It is for this reason that *halakha* has often been popularly defined as a "way" of life and that the goal is not abstract belief but "being Jewish" through action and performance. The basic fact that ideology and belief are carried by the *halakha* and its rituals and are not of much independent value is paradoxically expressed in an ancient rabbinic comment. It is there stated by God that he would rather that the people of Israel rejected him but continued to obey his Torah. Jewishness is therefore expressed not in theological abstractions, but in the ongoing acts of life, acts that suffuse the order of the day and establish the tempo and content of Judaism itself. Each act and gesture is thus part of a vast organic web of meaning and significance. The totality of all this is tradition.

The Life Cycle of Holiness

Rites of Passage

In addition to the recurrent daily and seasonal patterns of Judaism, the nonrecurrent moments of personal life are also given ritual distinction. These moments celebrate or mark times of new beginning and transition from one life stage to another. They dramatize the transience of individual existence, while highlighting those social symbols that give the community its identity and integrate the person into a larger sphere of meaning. Moments of passage are thus crucial in a double sense. First, while stressing the transience of life, they also provide the means of transcending this terror through the enduring symbols of religious meaning. Thus if the individual life is mortal, the ongoing community is a symbol of collective immortality and the permanence of values. Second, while stressing the transience of life, rites of passage also provide the means of transition from one life stage and one sphere of responsibility to another. They thus confirm the hierarchies of value of the community. And they also project an ideal sequence of personal development the individual can look forward to, so that, upon reaching each stage, a person can evaluate his or her maturation against a collective standard.

BIRTH

Birth is naturally the first major moment in a person's individual and communal life. When a boy is born, a circumcision rite called a *brit* ("covenant," short for *brit milah*, "covenant of circumcision") can be expected eight days later. This ceremony, of great antiquity, confirms the transition of the infant from being a child of Adam, as it were, to a member of the Jewish poeple. Thus the boy enters the "covenant of Abraham." The minor operation is delegated by the father to a ritually trained surgeon, called *mohel*. The *mohel* receives the child after he has been passed among the relatives, beginning with the mother (in a separate room; she is customarily secluded at this time). Just before the boy is given to the godfather (called *sandek*) to hold while the operation is performed according to the ancient procedure, the *mohel* temporarily places the child on a "chair of Elijah"—symbolic of the hopes of redemption. After the actual circumcision, the child is handed to the father (or an honored guest) while the *mohel* recites blessings in praise of God and for the welfare of the child. It is then that the boy's name is announced. The name (e.g., David son of Abraham) will be how the boy will be "called up" when he is honored to bless the Torah in later years; and this name will be marked upon his tombstone at death. Already from antiquity some Jews have had double names, a Hebrew name and a related vernacular name (e.g., in Hellenistic times one might be Jonathan or Matthew and Theodore, names all meaning "gift of God") or names that could function in both the ritual and secular communities. Among Ashkenazi Jews, it is customary to name the boy after a deceased relative; Sephardis, however, do not adhere to this practice. A joyous moment in the circumcision ceremony is when the entire assembly exclaims: "Just as he has entered the covenant, so may he enter [the study of] Torah, the wedding canopy, and good deeds." Thus a life cycle is outlined, which all the adults confirm through their own lives.

The naming ceremony for a girl traditionally takes place in the synagogue during a subsequent Sabbath service, when her father is "called up" to the Torah. In recent times in more liberal contexts, the mother is involved in this occasion, and new rituals for the birth of a girl have been developed. One of the more popular designations for these ceremonies is *simhat bat*, "joy [for the birth] of a daughter."

RELIGIOUS MAJORITY

The *study of Torah* traditionally begins quite early, for boys perhaps when they are three or four years old; and, according to custom, this event is inaugurated by having the child find and trace the letters of his name which are covered with honey. This act symbolizes the hopes for the sweetness of life devoted to Torah and the commandments. From youth, a boy will be instructed in Hebrew and the traditional classics of Judaism, but he will not be a formal member of the halakhic community until he is thirteen years old. At that time he will become a **bar mitzvah**, literally a "son of the commandment(s)." He can then perform all the *mitzvot* and is required to do so with full responsibility for his religious behavior. When the boy is first "called up" to the Torah, symbolic of his attainment of majority, the father utters a blessing commemorating this transition to adulthood.

A girl traditionally achieves majority at twelve years and a day, a time symbolic of reaching her menses, and is by then fully instructed in the intricacies of maintaining a ritually correct home, in the traditional rules of menstrual purity, and in some of the sacred texts. In recent times, girls are given fuller academic instruction in the traditional literature (though this varies by group) and in liberal contexts a *bat mitzvah* ceremony ("daughter of the commandment(s)") has been developed to mark the rite of passage. The degree to which this ceremony is part of the traditional service depends upon the strictness of the group. Some communities give a girl the same Torah ceremony as a boy; others only give her some ritual part in the Friday evening service; and still others limit this involvement to some celebratory action outside the framework of the *halakha*. There is naturally a high correlation between how a girl celebrates her majority status as a doer of *mitzvot* and the role of women in a given ritual community. Strict traditionalists, concerned with the separation of the sexes and the more minor ritual status of the female, will thus regard the moment as a female affair. Those groups that variously reject traditional rules about women (particularly matters of segregation in prayer, formal exclusion from the prayer quorum, and fewer required positive commandments) will correspondingly regard the moment of a girl's majority as a more ritual event along the lines enjoyed by males. Nowadays, such matters are subject to local rabbinic-communal regulation, though the communities themselves feel subject to the authority of different rabbinical institutions and their rulings on these halakhic matters.

MARRIAGE

For traditionalists and nontraditionalists alike, the wedding canopy is a major moment of personal and social transition. The male and female take their place as productive communal citizens and fulfill the first *mitzvah* of the Torah: to "be fruitful and multiply." The wedding is thus the transition to the basic Jewish institution of the home and to responsibility for the welfare of the community. In earlier times and still in some ultratraditional circles, marriages are arranged among peer groups. In such traditional groups, a bridegroom will not see his bride until near or on the wedding day; though nowadays when marriages are generally affected by more romantic inclinations and contact between groups is also more flexible, a period of acquaintance for the future couple is more common. Most modern traditionalists enjoy more flexible dating patterns, as do liberal Jews.

In Talmudic times, a stage of "betrothal" (*kiddushin* or *erusin*) preceded the "nuptuals" (*nisu'in*) by some time period. The two stages were combined in the post-Talmudic period and are celebrated together in the present Jewish wedding marriage ceremony. This latter formally begins in the afternoon (the bridegroom and bride having separately returned from ritual ablutions, a traditional practice), when the ancient contract formulas are reviewed by the "Arranger of *kiddushin*" and the document (*ketubbah*) is signed by witnesses. This *ketubbah* is read at the ceremony itself, along with seven blessings extolling the beauty of creation and the joys of companionship. The male will customarily wear his white *kittel* and recite the traditional marriage formula ("You are betrothed to me, with this ring, in accordance with the laws of Moses and Israel"). In Ashkenazi ceremonies, the couple shares wine and the groom breaks a glass. One explanation of this old custom is that it is a popular defense against evil spirits. Another interpretation gives a more moral explanation, saying that it recalls the sadness of the Temple's destruction in moments of joy. Among some Sephardis, the cup is smashed with wine in it as a sign of plenty. Related to such gestures of good omen, or *mazel tov*, it is customary to perform weddings at nightfall in view of the stars (which symbolize the divine promise to Abraham that his descendants would be as numerous as the stars); and on Tuesday (because of the double repetition in the biblical creation account of the phrase "and God saw that it was *good*" on that day). In certain periods associated with death or unfulfillment, marriages may not be performed.

It is considered a special *mitzvah* to praise the bride and entertain the groom. A whole repertoire of how one should dance before the bride and of the mirthful or mocking songs are part of the rich tradition linked to the event. In strictly traditional groups the dancing is performed by males and females in separate groups, and the bridegroom and bride are each hoisted up on chairs as the guests whirl roundabout. It is also customary to extend these festivities over a long period of time after the wedding day. Thus friends in different locales may invite the couple to a joyous reception where the seven blessings of the marriage ceremony are recited by honored guests. Torah teachings are given, and the *mitzvah* "to make the bridegroom rejoice in his bride" is fulfilled. Since the covenant at Sinai was imagined already by the ancient rabbis as a wedding between God and Israel, with the Torah as the *ketubbah* and Moses the "go-between," a deeper theological background is conveyed by the marriage occasion. The mystical understanding of the unity of male and female as symbolic of deeper divine and cosmic harmonies adds to the aura of the event.

DEATH

The consummate symbol of new social life, marriage, is indirectly linked to the final life stage, death. First, the white *kittel* the groom first wears on his wedding day will be his shroud, just as the prayer shawl (*tallit*) he receives at marriage is often used to form the bridal canopy and will be wrapped around him at death. Second, the children who are the manifestation of new family life will provide for social continuity after a parent's death and will be obliged to mourn for the dead parent and care for the other. And finally, just as a special meal is provided after the circumcision and wedding ceremonies, so is it customary for a "meal of consolation" to be provided the mourners by relatives and friends upon the return from the gravesite. In this way the transition to death is linked to symbols of social celebration and continuity.

Since death is the liminal moment par excellence, dramatizing the ultimate changes of status for the deceased and relatives, and because the occasion of death is one of great anxiety and disrupts established social patterns, all the procedures connected with the event are carefully regulated by the *halakha* or fixed custom. There are thus several post mortem periods that require different actions by the living. These periods have traditionally been correlated with the stages of departure of the deceased's soul and are recognized by different terms.

The period between death and burial (usually within three days) is the first stage. Upon hearing of the death of near kin, the mourner (now called *onen*) rips his or her garments and acknowledges God as "the true Judge." Great restrictions are imposed upon the *onen*. Shaving, the wearing of leather, and certain types of washing are forbidden. He or she recites psalms, is exempt from most positive commandments, and makes sure that the body of the deceased is ritually purified and dressed in a shroud (earth from the land of Israel is customarily placed in the simple wood coffin for those dying "in exile"). "Watchers" stay awake with the corpse and recite psalms. After the burial ceremony and the first recitation of the **kaddish** prayer (a glorification of God's power and redemptive help), the second mourning stage begins. It is called *shiva* ("seven," in Hebrew), for this mourning period lasts seven days. From this time on the mourner is known as an *avel*. Near relatives stay together at the home of one for the week and customarily sit on low seats. During daily prayers performed in the house of the mourner certain prayers are deleted and psalms added. Consolation is bestowed by the community by visiting the bereaved after morning prayers, or before or after evening ones. This is considered an important *mitzvah*. Customarily a visitor will not initiate conversation with an *avel*, respecting the mourner's private mood; and if a conversation is started, it is considered proper to restrict the topic to the merits of the deceased. Upon departing from an *avel*, one says (in Hebrew): "May the Almighty comfort you, together with all the mourners of Zion and Jerusalem."

After *shiva* the mourner returns to normal activities, though refraining from celebrations (also haircutting and newly pressed clothes) for thirty days. During this period (the third stage), too, and for eleven months thereafter (the fourth stage), the *kaddish* is recited in communal services. Throughout this period, the mourner will not sit in his or her customary seat in the synagogue—another sign of this liminal period. This stage closes with the unveiling of the tombstone. On the anniversary of death according to the Jewish calendar (called in Yiddish *Yahrzeit*) and during subsequent holy days when special memorial recitations occur, the former mourner again rises to recite the *kaddish*. During the *Yahrzeit* for a relative, the male will often be honored with leading communal prayer. In some circles, it is also customary to hire someone to recite the *kaddish* for the deceased if this would not otherwise be done. Such prayers for the "souls of the departed," that they "find rest in the Presence of the Almighty," are thus of important emotional and ritual significance.

Through such periodic memorials the dead are not "cut off" from the community. Moreover, as noted earlier, ancestors are remembered by having their names given to newborns and by visitation to gravesites before Rosh Hashanah (also on the *Yahrzeit*). In addition, martyrs of the past are remembered on Sabbaths and holy days and graves of saints or sages of the past have often been sites of pilgrimage—pilgrims pray there for divine blessing through the intercession of this "righteous holy one" in Heaven. The graves of Rachel and the patriarchs in the land of Israel have been places of prayer and pilgrimage for certain Ashkenazis, especially Hasidim; and *hilula* ceremonies at the tombs of sages and relatives are still common among Sephardi Jews. In recent years, the deathcamps where Jews were murdered in Europe during World War II have been the locale of memorial pilgrimages, as also the Yad Va-Shem shrine in Israel. The power of the memory of ancestors and persecution are thus very dominant in Jewish life and pervade the consciousness of Jews at different levels the year round.

Crisis Rituals

If the ordinary cycle of Jewish life is something on the order of "one continuous worship service with minor interruptions," personal and communal crises engage another level of ritual behavior. In highly traditional circles, from antiquity to recent times, a whole range of popular and often officially sanctioned (though not always halakhic) behaviors have been practiced. Thus ancient Talmudic spells and medieval and later magical recipes (like those found in the tract *The Angel Raziel*) have been used to ward off evil spirits at childbirth or special occasions, to promote fertility and counteract disease, and to dispel the effects of a bad dream. Among other crisis rituals still practiced in some traditional circles, one may particularly mention the practice of fasting in the wake of a bad dream. Such self-imposed fasts are regulated by halakhic norms. Another still common act is the custom of changing the name of a gravely ill or dying person in the hope that the new name will inaugurate a new lease on life (and also "trick" the Angel of Death into believing that the moribund person has died). Even persons who have otherwise little link to such nonrational procedures may nevertheless perform them as a gesure of desperation or hope. In a similar way, the custom of placing notes with petitions at the gravesite of a holy ancestor or especially of placing them in the cracks of the so-called Wailing Wall of the ancient Temple in Jerusalem is still common among Jews of all persuasions. For some, this act is of great supernatural benefit; for others, it remains a folk custom or charm—but one not to be disregarded for all that.

The performers of crisis rituals vary with the halakhic status of the acts. Thus, in medieval times individuals might divine their own daily fate through forms of bibliomancy (randomly examining biblical passages, especially the psalms); or, in particularly dire circumstances, they might have recourse to the special prayers and charms of a midwife or rabbi. On the other hand, rituals against drought, plague, or persecution affecting the entire community were integrated into the halakhic format of daily life and given official sanction, just as the crisis of martyrdom (called *kiddush ha-Shem*, "Sanctification of the Divine Name") was also a halakhically regulated procedure for both group and individual. In premodern times it was also quite common, in the face of natural or historical disasters, for persons to undertake great acts of penitence involving self-mortification but also almsgiving "to avert the severe decree." It must therefore be noted that in the history of Judaism crisis rituals were not only of a personal and self-centered nature, but they also involved special acts for the welfare of the community. Even more, in late medieval mystical groups especially, the supernatural dimension of the natural or historical crisis was the main focus of attention. And so rituals designed "to repair" a cosmic crisis or imbalance affecting human life below were performed with great passion and conviction. In all these ways and at all these levels, crisis rituals demonstrate the powerful function of ritual actions to order and sustain one's personal or social world.

The Social Circles of Holiness

The rituals of Jewish life typically occur in several expanding spheres, though the boundaries are not always firmly fixed between them and most activities can occur in all spheres. Thus, to move from the home to the synagogue does not mean that personal prayer is restricted to the home and group prayer to the synagogue or that table fellowship and study are greatly different in either place. Similarly, to move beyond these two spheres to the wider communal realm does not mean that the legal aspects of life or acts of charity are restricted to this latter domain. Nevertheless, each sphere (home, synagogue, and community) is a special locus involving distinct types of social interaction and frames of mind. They therefore require separate consideration.

Family and Home

Traditionally, the home is the nuclear holy space and the family the nuclear ritual unit of Judaism. To the doorpost at the right of entry a Jew affixes a **mezuzah**, a case with a Hebrew parchment on which the biblical Shema passage is inscribed. The *mezuzah* is thus an external sign that the house is "Jewish" and a symbol of the Jewish values and behavior espoused inside. Today most Jews continue this custom even if the home life is largely nonhalakhic. The *mezuzah* thus functions partially as a good-luck charm and loose badge of social identity. In more traditional homes, the *mezuzah* functions as a holy object separating the outside "profane" from the inside "sacred" space. Crossing the threshold (and venerating the *mezuzah* by touching it and kissing one's hand) is thus a ritual act: a movement inward, from the world to the distinctly Jewish domain.

Here, in the home, the dominant value is *shalom bayit* ("the peace of the home"), regulated by strong codes of parental respect and hierarchy. Honoring one's parents is a child's duty of great importance, a *mitzvah* advocated even in the most trying circumstances. Correspondingly, care for one's children, including educational and financial support, is considered a primary parental duty. Such patterns of respect and hierarchy are customarily expressed in many ways, but particularly at table. Children do not sit in their parents' chairs, eat before parents say the blessing over food, or leave the table until parents conclude grace after meals. This hierarchy is somewhat disrupted during the Passover, when children inaugurate the *seder* rite with questions and songs, but it is also more fluidly interrupted at all family moments of ritual sharing, when the children are given acts of honor and involvement.

The table, compared earlier to an altar, dominates the home for festive and daily occasions. The food eaten is traditionally *kasher* (colloquially, **kosher**; i.e., halakhically "proper") in terms of the dietary regulations involved. Crustaceans and pork (among other "fish" and land animals) are prohibited by biblical law, and mixtures of dairy and flesh products (so-called milk and meat; colloquially, *milchig* and *fleishig*) are prohibited by rabbinic law. Moreover, permitted land animals (like cows, also fowl) must be ritually slaughtered by special procedures that include soaking and salting the meat so as to drain off the blood.

Accordingly, all table fellowship is at the same time ritual fellowship. The related consideration is that, because of strict adherence to these regulations, strictly traditional Jews will not eat in gentile homes or allow "nonkosher" food into their own. Thus, ritual fellowship determines table fellowship. In this way, food becomes a symbol of social difference and group maintenance. In modern times, minor gradations of observance of the ancient dietary rules are common, so that some traditional Jews will eat dairy or vegetable food outside the home under certain circumstances. The use of public (nonkosher) restaurants for such purposes is thus, further, a statement about one's halakhic position on these matters. Symbolically, where and how one eats extend the domain of the home and structure the types of personal contact one will have. For this reason, some lenient moderns may observe forms of dietary propriety (*kashrut*) at home but be more flexible outside, thereby indicating that their Jewishness is a "private matter" only. Observance of traditional food rules is thus a key indicator of a Jew's overall halakhic observance and general attitude towards assimilation to non-Jewish patterns.

The Synagogue

In traditional Jewish life, the synagogue has functioned as a house of prayer, a house of study, and a place of communal assembly. All these functions are interrelated (since gathering together for prayer includes the hearing or recitation of sacred texts; and the study of sacred texts commonly occurs in gatherings in prayer rooms). Because of this close relationship between prayer and study, the synagogue is colloquially (in the Ashkenazi sphere) referred to as Shul

Great Leningrad Synagogue. Jews may gather for a prayer quorum in homes, special build-ings or in nature. Synagogue architecture has varied with place and time. The Torah Ark is at the eastern side. Photo credit: Bill Aron.

(*Shul* is a Yiddish word for synagogue *and* school). Moreover, "to go to Shul," in the common parlance, may mean to gather in the synagogue for prayer, for study, or for fellowship.

The synagogue is thus the center of the traditional Jewish com-munity, the shared building and symbolic home for all. In its formal seating structures (the traditional segregation of male and female or the less traditional integration of male and female), in its informal seating patterns, and in its political structures and system of ritual honors, the Shul dramatizes the public values and social hierarchies of the particular community. Moreover, because traditional Jews are halakhically prohibited from driving on the Sabbath and festivals, they tend to live in close proximity to one another and to the Shul. This factor further heightens their social interdependence. Indeed, the fairly restricted nature of this reference group for esteem and fel-lowship has tended to encourage halakhic conformity and social propriety among the members. Formally, rabbinic scholars and the halakhically pious dominate the hierarchy of the traditional com-munity; but the wealthy "householder" and the bestowers of syna-gogue honors have always exerted great informal social control. In less traditional circles, where driving is permitted (at the least to attend Sabbath or festival services), the synagogue is not within the near radius of all homes; and so it is also not the only place where members may interact communally. In these circumstances, the range of values and patterns of social evaluation are more varied and tend to conform to the social and value hierarchies of the wider society.

Nevertheless, to be a "Shul-goer" (or synagogue- or temple-goer) is somewhat synonymous with being a practicing Jew in accordance with the halakhic norms of one's immediate community. Synagogue membership is thus an assumed pattern of association where one can fulfill communal halakhic obligations, become more knowledgeable about Jewish life and culture, and generally mingle with other Jews who share similar life-styles and values. Nowadays, in areas of great Jewish population density, there is an obvious correlation between how close one lives to a synagogue and the degree to which Jewish behaviors and attitudes are central. In the less populous Jewish areas of modern America, membership in a synagogue will be maintained even at great distances, since it not only provides for occasional ritual needs but expresses needs of ethnic-social identity as well.

The Community

As we have seen, a number of Jewish values are expressed in and through halakhic behaviors. Thus one is obliged to feed guests and give them shelter, to give charity to the poor and maintain Jewish charitable institutions, to help needy Jews worldwide through financial and political intercession, and to return lost objects and visit the sick. All these are fixed halakhic obligations, or *mitzvot*. But they may also tend to have a superhalakhic dimension too, for to say that it is a *mitzvah* to do the above behaviors does not simply imply them to be commandments, but the "right thing"—something that transcends individual convenience or personal satisfaction. Thus when a Jew says that "it is a *mitzvah*" to help the poor or to be just, he or she means that such acts are dominating values that take precedence over all else whenever the occasion arises. Moreover, to say that some behavior "is a *mitzvah*" is to give that act the ultimate authority and motivation. It is to say that it derives from the official code of Jewish behavior and that it is an essential feature of it. Today, when nontraditional Jews explain their involvement in social causes, philanthropic associations, or politically related Jewish activities, they may refer to such work as "a *mitzvah*." By this they regard their actions as "Jewish" in some sense and as expressive of their "Jewishness." Further, they tend to see their actions as expressions of Jewish moral teachings and their devotion to this work as "religious" in some sense. For this reason, many such moderns feel with strong conviction that in performing acts of Jewish communal service, they are "good Jews," though in traditional circles and in more formal terms this attribution is not a moral evaluation but a halakhic one, bestowed upon one who conforms to the halakhic consensus.

The obligation to work for the community is thus a traditional Jewish value with broad modern nuances. In fact, for Jews, there is no social value higher than "love of the people Israel" (*ahavat Yisrael*)—concern for the welfare of all Jews. Social factors of isolation, memories of persecution, and the historical need for communal self-reliance have certainly contributed to this. Nevertheless, the holy texts of Judaism, from the Bible on, together with the traditional daily liturgy all express the firm belief that the God of Israel is the Creator of all and that all creatures descend from Adam. Accordingly, the wider moral category of "love of fellow creatures" (*ahavat ha-beriyot*) as well as the ideals of universal peace and reconciliation remain essential and repeated traditional values in Judaism. The liberal wing of modern Judaism has promoted universal concerns to a preeminent status in its religious ideology. In this, such liberal Jews have kept the conscience of Judaism attuned to its ancient ideals.

■

CHAPTER IV

Jews and Judaism in Modern Times

At the conclusion of our historical discussion in Chapter II, various changes affecting Jews and Judaism in modern times were considered. Central among these were transformations of a social and psychological nature, the increased decentralization of Torah, and the revival of Jewish nationalism. While these developments may be seen as separate phenomena, they are also deeply interrelated. The splintering of medieval Jewish communal and religious structures increasingly exposed Jews to the varieties of general culture around them and to such liberal concerns as natural reason and natural rights. For those subject to these influences, virtually nothing was left unexamined and virtually everything was subject to choice or decision. Should one remain a Jew and in what way? Is Judaism compatible with "general culture," or should it be changed? Are Scripture and rabbinic literature the only authoritative texts, or might one be instructed by literary creations from other cultures? And finally, should Judaism be one's only or primary loyalty or might there be other groups with compelling claims upon one's moral or religious sensibilities?

These and many more questions circulated among Jews from the mid-eighteenth century on. As noted earlier, some pockets of Jewry resisted change, but nowhere was the decision to change or to resist taken without thought or care. Everyone had to make a choice of some kind. Accordingly, the modern world for Jews is characterized by the pressure of just this option: either to resist the power of tradition and commit oneself to a new and larger world or to resist the new ideas of modernity as threats to traditional truths and forms.

Of course, only at the radical edges of the spectrum was the choice posed in such a polar way. Most Jews were more compromising, although these solutions were also asserted in manifesto-like forms in the early period.

The processes and possibilities set in motion in the eighteenth century are still very much part of Judaism today. Indeed, two hundred years is a comparatively short span of time within which responses to the modern assault on two thousand years of tradition might be worked out. In this sense, Judaism is still deeply involved in the dynamic of its "reformation," and the emergent shapes are still very much in flux in both traditional and nontraditional circles. To gain some sense of this variety, we shall first focus on several expressions found in two European cities and then on several others in two different countries, Israel and the United States. The examples are typical of the times and their temper.

A Tale of Two Cities: Vilna and Frankfurt am Main

Vilna

Soon after receiving the rights of settlement in the sixteenth century, the Jews of Vilna (now Vilnius), Lithuania, quickly established that city as the preeminent center of traditional Talmudic piety in northern Europe. Its stature reached unparalled heights in modern Jewish life through the example of Rabbi Elijah ben Solomon. Also known as "The Gaon (Eminence, Genius) of Vilna," Rabbi Elijah Gaon was born in or near Vilna in 1720 and died in that city in 1797. He has been called the "last great theologian of classical rabbinism"; and in the context of the new ritual and ideological developments of his day, Rabbi Elijah took his stand as a staunch, authoritarian supporter of Jewish medieval tradition. Rigidly and censoriously he resisted any deviance from the old Jewish norms. As one of the last towering figures of Talmudic rabbinism, the Gaon of Vilna became a symbol of resistance to "unauthorized change" in Judaism (that is, change not authorized by certain ultratraditionalists) as well as a model of devotion to tradition and its comprehensive truth claims.

Born to a distinguished family of scholars, Elijah ben Solomon was quickly recognized as a child prodigy when he had mastered the Bible and traversed "the sea of the Talmud" by the age of six. As a youth, he mastered the *Zohar*, practiced various mystical-magical behaviors, and expanded his interests to include mathematics, astronomy, and botany. He mastered all these disciplines on his own (for Jews were not part of any public educational system) in an attempt to comprehend his Jewish sources. For him, "everything that was, is, and will be is included in the Torah—and not only principles, but even the details of each species, the minutest details of each creature, plant, and mineral." According to Rabbi Baruch of Shklov in the introduction to his translation of Euclid done at the request of the Gaon (1780), Rabbi Elijah said that "to the degree that a man is lacking in knowledge of secular sciences he will lack one-hundred-fold in the wisdom of the Torah." Here then is a unique ideology for the use of Western science *in the service of the truth of Torah*.

The productive output of the Gaon's learning is astonishing. Over seventy scholarly books and pamphlets have been attributed to him. Some he penned himself, while others were culled from the marginalia he inscribed on his copies of classical texts or from the lecture notes of his faithful disciples. He was a profound annotator of virtually every book in the rich traditional library of Judaism: the Bible, the Mishnah and Tosephta, the Babylonian and Jerusalem Talmuds, the volumes of legal and homiletical *midrash*, assorted mystical texts (like the mystical-cosmological *Sepher Yetzirah* or obscure sections of the *Zohar*), and the legal codes (like the *Shulkhan Arukh*). He even wrote on Hebrew grammar in the medieval style. His all-absorbing and fanatical dedication to the truth of Jewish texts led Rabbi Elijah to become a scholarly and religious ascetic, who lived in his home with the shutters boarded up, studying by candlelight so as not to know if it was day or night. According to the testimony of his son, the Gaon never slept more than two hours a day and even then never more than a half hour at a time. Such was the stuff of legend, to be sure; but similar examples of scholarly devotion to the divine word are known from earlier ages and in the practices of sages of more recent times.

It may be because Rabbi Elijah had become an independent scholar at such an early age that he was remarkably free of the style of complex Talmudic dialectics (called *pilpul*) then still in vogue in Poland and Lithuania and was able to develop his own critical style of rabbinic study. Indeed, for all his traditionalism, the Gaon in a way paradoxically anticipates features of the modern critical study of the Talmud. For him, the primary condition for textual criticism was a disciplined reason, with no reliance upon the opinions of earlier authorities. In the course of his study, the Gaon became aware of what would later be called "lower textual criticism," for he came to realize that many older laws or formulations were based upon passages that had become corrupted in the course of their scribal transmission. He thus sought to restore original textual readings by conjectural emendations that are feats of intuitive genius. By this means he hoped that the *halakha* would be firmly established upon the basis of the "original" readings of the sources, not upon the accumulated errors of their copyists. The Gaon was also involved in what would later be called "higher textual criticism," for he was also aware of discrepancies between parallel formulations of halakhic rules in the Mishnah and Tosephta or between the Babylonian and Jerusalem Talmuds, and he tried to resolve them and deal with such issues as their relative historical priority. Since the goal of all this

Talmud study is a sacred obligation, performed alone or in study groups and often in the local synagogue. Talmud study is at the core of the traditional rabbinical curriculum. The Talmud is learned with an oral, singing recitation. Photo credit: Bill Aron.

study was to plumb the depths of divine Truth, Rabbi Elijah's rigor was ruthless and his independent spirit a subject of awe.

In all his ways the Gaon of Vilna was a distinct personality. And, as remarked, he represented the old path of traditional rabbinism in the face of the many new currents then swirling about in the Jewish world. A brief glance at the world to the west and east of Vilna in his day will bring out this point.

Glancing westward toward Berlin, we see Moses Mendelssohn (1729–1786) living among the rational philosophers and advocating the study of nontraditional subjects for spiritual and cultural development. Like his fellow Maskilim ("Enlightened Ones"), he felt that the old curriculum of learning was not sufficient for the proper cultivation of the human "spirit" or for furthering the integration of the Jews into the larger cultural mainstream of Europe. Clearly for Mendelssohn, unlike the Gaon, "everything" was *not* "included in the Torah." Moreover, he did not consider the Torah to be the *revealed* source of eternal truths. As a philosopher of the times, Mendelssohn distinguished between a religion of reason and empirical teachings. The truths of reason are eternal and open to all persons and they are not dependent upon a special revelation. Empirical teachings, on the other hand, are temporal truths of fact and subject to ongoing experience. So viewed, the Torah of Judaism is not unique for its eternal truths (which are accessible through reason to all), but rather because it contains revealed laws that guide and formally constitute the Jewish polity. As Mendelssohn argued in his book *Jerusalem* (1783), this polity exists no longer, so that the modern Jew is thoroughly a citizen of the secular state and *its* legislative constraints. For Mendelssohn and for his circle, religion was thus a private and inward matter; they argued that as long as people conformed to the outward public good there must be tolerance for divergent religions and their practices. Variations on this theme have resounded in modern Western religious life, both Jewish and non-Jewish.

The Gaon of Vilna never publicly turned against the Maskilim, perhaps because those of his day still remained observant Jews. But he could not have disagreed more strongly with their more diminished notion of Torah and their advocacy of secular study. Nor would he have appreciated the irony that his style of textual criticism would be developed in succeeding generations among Jews who advocated the "Scientific Study of Judaism" for the sake of pure historical reconstruction as well as as a means of demonstrating the cultural richness of Judaism to Christians. Much closer to home, it was rather the ways of the Hasidim that evoked Rabbi Elijah's ire. Now since the Hasidim were observant Jews who also believed in the mystic and absolute truth of Torah, the Gaon's hostility to them must be traced to the threat this new movement posed to traditional structures of rabbinic authority.

As noted earlier, Hasidism developed patterns of charismatic authority and often demoted Torah study before such values as group and individual mystical experience. To the strict Talmudic traditionalists, these features reawakened memories of the failed messianic movement (led by the apostate Sabbatai Tzvi) that had rocked Jewry a century earlier. They were thus vigilant against any new expressions of nonconformist behavior in Judaism. In addition, there was also anger at some new variations introduced by the Hasidim into the liturgy and ritual slaughter. The combination of these factors, experienced at intense emotional levels, induced the Jews of Vilna to draw the Gaon into the thickening fray and issue edicts of excommunication against their fellow Jews. Given the animosity of the edicts and counteredicts over a long time, it is not the least of historical ironies that the new changes brought on by modernity eventually produced an unofficial alliance between the Hasidim and their erstwhile "opponents" (called Mitnaggedim) against the "godless secularists" or reformers. A further irony is that, in more recent times, the Hasidim have themselves emerged as the last bastion of conservative orthodoxy and regularly issue edicts against both the "godless" and other (even ultra-) traditionalists who deviate from their norms.

Let us return to Vilna. One of the Gaon's celebrated students, Rabbi Hayyim ben Isaac, sought to reinvigorate traditional life and piety with a new *yeshiva* (rabbinic academy) established near Vilna, in Volozhin. Founded in 1803, it became one of the most celebrated academies of Talmudic rationalism in the nineteenth century and contributed generations of rabbis to Jewish life until it was closed by the Russian government in 1892. A brief glimpse of the daily schedule in the *yeshiva* may give some indication of the structural pattern of a traditional Talmudic study regime and its passionate dedication and rigor.

The official day began with the morning *shaharit* prayers at 8 A.M., after which the students (which Rabbi Hayyim refered to as "the men of the *yeshiva*") had breakfast. Following this, the weekly portion of the Torah was studied and explained along with traditional commentaries by the principal. Study of the Talmud (and later commentaries and codes) then proceeded in groups (which Rabbi Hayyim preferred to self-study) from 10 A.M. to 1 P.M. After this, a major lecture was given. In the 1880s the lecture during the first part of the week was given by Rabbi Hayyim Soloveitchik and in the second half of the week by Rabbi Naftali Tzvi Berlin, both renowned for their incisive Talmudic analyses. Following the lecture, the noonday meal was taken and the students were free until 4 P.M., when the afternoon *minhah* prayers were recited. Students then studied until 10 P.M., when the evening *ma'ariv* prayers were conducted and supper followed. Most students would then return to the *yeshiva* to study until midnight. They would then sleep until 3 A.M., when they would return to their benches to study until morning prayers. The method of study cultivated in the *yeshiva* was intense scrutiny of the Talmudic text and independent "straight thinking" (not excessive logical pyrotechnics). The ideal was *torah li-shemah,* study for the sake of pure understanding. According to Rabbi Hayyim, Torah study was a form of direct communion with God. Among the "men of the *yeshiva*," such study was combined with a strong emphasis on the objective performance of the commandments and a corresponding derogation of their subjective, experiential component (the Hasidic way). Students would remain for years in this intense atmosphere, and they were examined by the principal once each term.

The atmosphere of scholarly diligence and piety at the Eitz Hayyim *yeshiva* in Volozhin became legendary. Among the famous glorifications of such Talmudic asceticism and devotion was a poem written by one of its former students, the modern Jewish poet laureate Hayyim Nahman Bialik (1873–1934). In "The Eternal Student" and "On the Threshold of the House of Study," Bialik sings nostalgically of the faithful dedication of such divine service, a service that required the student to sublimate all feelings for nature and beauty for the sake of a single-minded devotion to the spiritual ideal. He recognized that this devotion had "formed the heart of the nation." But, like others of his generation who began to read widely in Western culture, the exclusivity of Talmud study and the fixed patterns of traditional Jewish life seemed narrow and repressive. Nostalgia was thus coupled with anger and rejection. The ancient theme of the Temple service (which we have repeatedly touched upon in these pages) is symptomatic of these changes. Bialik likens the house of study to the Temple of old and the decay of the ideals of traditional learning and self-sacrifice to the destruction of the ancient Shrine. Faced with this new loss and in despair over the loss of faith, Bialik exhorts an entire generation to return to Zion and rebuild their ancient homeland. In a speech delivered at the opening of the Hebrew University in Jerusalem (1925), the poet likened the new builders of the land to the priests of the Temple. The new "service" was thus devotion to the renewal of national culture on a spiritual foundation. In this regard, Bialik worked tirelessly to revive the Hebrew language, reedit national religious classics in new forms for the modern imagination, and help establish educational institutions that would implement the ancient ideals of Judaism in new ways.

Bialik emigrated from Russia to the land of Israel and settled in the new city of Tel Aviv in solidarity with the new centers of creativity and work the pioneers had established throughout the land. Jerusalem was the ancient holy city, representing the traditional Zionist longings of millennia; Tel Aviv, the "Mound of Spring," was to be the symbol of the new Zionism, of the self-created life in the homeland with its ideals of a return to nature and physical labor. Thus, if the ancient Temple ideals of *avodah* (shrinal "service" and work) had been transformed over the centuries to include divine "service" through study and observance of the commandments, this term was utterly transformed in early Zionism to refer to physical "work" on the land. *Avodah* now became "service" to the nation and the national-spiritual renewal through productive and self-reliant "work." Indeed, this was the new form of "worship" for all those Jewish pioneers for whom the ancient faith no longer made a truth claim upon them, but who nevertheless remained Jews in both spirit and sensibility. Some of the new "returnees to Zion" were, in fact, aggressive secularists concerned to restore a lost national connectedness to the cycles of nature (from ancient Canaanite and Israelite times). Others sought to transmute the spiritual teachings of the past into new forms—a sort of cultural alchemy. But all were dedicated to transforming the old "*galut* Jew" into a new breed, into a self-reliant actor in history, into a person devoted to physical and moral renewal in the homeland. In waves, the idealists and the oppressed on the ancient nation "went up" to the land "to build and be rebuilt in it" (as an early "work song" had it), just as generations before "went up" to the Temple and Torah service. The old word *aliyah* (the act of "going up") thus took on a thoroughly new meaning.

Through the reinterpretation of old religious symbols like *avodah*, through a renewal of the ancient ideal of a return to the ancestral homeland, and through the reapplication of traditional texts, Zionism is in many respects a continuation and new expression of the Jewish religious spirit. Even a staunch traditionalist like Rabbi Abraham Isaac ha-Cohen Kook (1865–1935), the Ashkenazi chief rabbi of the land of Israel from 1921 to his death, recognized this and regularly intervened with the ultra-traditionalists on behalf of the secularists. Also a product of the Volozhin *yeshiva* and an almost exact contemporary of Bialik, Rabbi Kook understood the national awakening in traditional messianic terms and saw the socialist pioneers as the spiritual vanguard of the nation. In a famous defense of the secularists, Kook stressed that when the ancient Temple was being built even ordinary "workers" could stand where, later, only the high priest could "serve." Traditionalists, he argued, should see through the external expressions of the "builders" to the deep "love of Israel" that motivated them. A profound reinterpreter of the mystical tradition, Kook worked for unity at all levels of human life. He sought to fan the "sparks of holiness" wherever they glimmered and to build through them a "new light in Zion." In his great theological work *Lights of Holiness* (three volumes), Rabbi Kook retaught the ideals of devoted service to God and the need to enhance the divine creative force in all things. This is a redemptive task he felt would unify the Jewish people. His goal was thus a renewal of stultified traditionalism and a transformation of traditionless secularism through the energy of a common national *avodah* in the holy land. The unification of Jews in Zion actively devoted to peace and divine creativity would, he believed, be "the beginning of the (ultimate) redemption" that he, as a traditional Jew, awaited in faith. Rabbi Kook inspired a generation of religious and nonreligious Zionists alike.

Frankfurt am Main

A different range of modern Jewish expression is exemplified by various personalities of the western European city of Frankfurt am Main. Jews had frequented the annual fall fairs of this city from 1074 on and had developed there a distinct set of ritual procedures. Prayer books still mention the "rites of Frankfurt" along with the standard Ashkenazi and Sephardi rites. Frankfurt Jewry developed during the Middle Ages and, by the mid-nineteenth century, boasted major Orthodox and Reform rabbis. In subsequent decades, Frankfurt was also the scene of major moments in modern Jewish life and thought.

Among the distinguished citizens of Frankfurt am Main was Abraham Geiger (1810–1874), who was a leading proponent of Liberal-Reform Judaism and served as a communal rabbi there between 1863 and 1870. He was one of the great founders and contributors to the "Scientific Study of Judaism" movement as well, and through his historical researches in the biblical text and the liturgy he gave support to the liberal view that Judaism was an evolving religious civilization. He opposed orthodoxy, which he judged to have become ossified and unasthetic and was among the proponents of a Jewish "mission" to spread rational faith in One God and his moral teachings. Geiger strived, like other reformers of the time, to turn Judaism solely into a religious community and eliminate all features that would separate Jews from the gentile nations. He thus advocated praying in the vernacular (and not Hebrew), removing references to a "return to Zion" from the prayer book, and changing prayer formulations that no longer reflected current beliefs (thus the ancient prayer that God was "reviver of the dead" was changed to refer to him as the "source of eternal life"). Also, like other reformers before and since, he permitted instrumental music in the synagogue service and was lenient regarding some forms of Sabbath work. However, he opposed changing the Sabbath from Saturday to Sunday and rejected proposals to abolish the rite of circumcision.

Geiger met his future Orthodox adversary Rabbi Samson Raphael Hirsch (1808-1888) at the university in Bonn (1829) while both were students there in ancient languages and history. Though Hirsch was a product of a traditional Talmudic education, he was also influenced by the more enlightened wing of Orthodoxy that countenanced the study of Western culture. Indeed, one of the famous bywords associated with Hirsch and that influenced generations of Orthodox Jews was "Torah with *derekh eretz*," "the (traditional) study of Torah *with* secular studies." In addition, as a communal rabbi (he served in Frankfurt from 1851 to 1888), Hirsch introduced some liturgical adjustments (like adding a choir and preaching occasionally in the vernacular).

Nevertheless, Rabbi Hirsch was an opponent of Reform Judaism. In his theological work *Nineteen Letters* (1836), he not only stated that Judaism is an expression of God's will through the Torah but, by emphasizing that the Torah is a feature of divine truth and *not* dependent upon society, he diminished the significance of historical process as a factor affecting the development of Judaism. Such an attitude was rejected by Geiger and this led to a split between the former friends. Moreover, Hirsch's notion that Judaism is not solely a religious community but a "national religious consciousness" whose mission it is to teach the nations "that God is the source of blessing" further divided him from Geiger and reformist ideology. Indeed, for him the cultivation of *Menschentum* (Ger., "humanity") is but a preparatory stage in the development of *Israeltum* (Ger., "Jewishness"), whereby one is truly led to perfection. These ideas had (and still have) a great impact on Orthodox Jewish life. Hirsch propagated them from the pulpit, through such popular forums as the *Jeschurun* journal, which he edited, and in his Bible translation and exegesis. The latter was based on traditional notions of revelation and, because of Hirsch's denial that Jewish values and ideals had a historical development, rejected the critical approach to biblical interpretation then making headway in the universities of Europe.

In some respects, the difference between Hirsch's Orthodoxy and Geiger's Liberalism is the difference between those (the Orthodox) who would argue for the a priori nature of Jewish belief and practice, regarding such as the "objective given" to which subjective attitudes must conform, and those (the Liberals) who would argue for the a priori nature of historical subjectivity, regarding Jewish belief and practice as a product of human experience. A more mediating position is represented by Franz Rosenzweig, who was born in Cassel, Germany, in 1886 and died in Frankfurt in 1929. He typifies the estranged modern Jew, the product of Western culture, who could nevertheless return to a vital and unapologetic Jewish life *beyond Liberalism and Orthodoxy*. For many contemporaries, the model of his intellectual transformation and the model of his piety and integrity during years of a degenerative illness have transfigured the life of Rosenzweig into the story of a modern saint and sage.

Franz Rosenzweig did not start his religious journey from within a firm Jewish center. A highly assimilated home that only minimally conformed to the outer trappings of Judaism, Rosenzweig's family was more attuned to the values and concerns of the *Frankfurter Zeitung*, an influential upper-class newspaper of the time, than to Jewish tradition. As for many others, this attitude was not especially marked by a hostile rejection of Jewish ideology. It was simply based on the fact that Judaism no longer appeared as a vital spiritual force and so simply faded into the background before other interests.

Rosenzweig himself studied history, medicine, and philosophy and eventually produced the significant *Hegel and the State*. But already as a youth, shortly before World War I, he keenly felt the need for a vital religious life. And so, along with several other friends, Rosenzweig considered conversion to Christianity. After long probing, he determined to enter the church in the way advocated by the earliest Christian missionaries to the Jews—as a Jew, not as a pagan. In the course of his preparations, he visited a small Orthodox synagogue in Berlin during the high holy days of 1913. Rosenzweig emerged from the Yom Kippur service with the decision to remain a Jew. As he expressed it in a powerful exchange of letters with Eugen Rosenstock, Judaism was not an antiquated or parochial religion without vibrancy in the modern age. Moreover, he, a born Jew, had no need to come to God the Father through the Son, as did the pagans, for he was *already* with the Father. Redemption and nearness to God are always immediately available to the Jew, he maintained; no mediation is necessary. But he added, this does not mean that Judaism is superior to Christianity and will replace it in some ultimate future; neither does Christianity, for its part, fulfill or negate Judaism. Both ways are true; both Judaism and Christianity are two valid expressions of religious truth and will remain so until the final redemption. Until that time, Jews must maintain their eternal, community-centered life of religious observance, inwardly regenerating like the fire of the sun, while Christians will continue to be the sun's rays, outwardly extending in time and space to convert the unbeliever to God. In his idea of a "double covenant," according theological validity to Christianity and challenging this religion to a reciprocal acknowledgement of Judaism, Rosenzweig parted company with almost all Jewish thinkers before him. His position opened the way to the possibility of genuine interreligious dialogue—without the triumphalist pride of either group and without hidden agendas of conversion.

Rosenzweig came to reject German idealist philosophy, which regarded concrete experience as secondary to pure thought. For Rosenzweig, true thinking is not abstracted from life, but is deeply a part of it, beginning with the awareness of personal death and the uniqueness of each human life. This is the core of his celebrated "New Thinking," a type of commonsense theology that explored the concreteness of life lived with the awareness of death. Stationed on the Balkan front during World War I, Rosenzweig wrote out his religious thoughts on postcards that were sent home and subsequently published in 1921 under the title *The Star of Redemption*. In this theological masterwork, he fully developed his religious existentialism or, better, coexistentialism, for he believed that the individual person was never alone, but always working out his or her destiny with God.

For Rosenzweig, the truth of Judaism lies precisely in the capacity of its categories and behaviors to aid one to live dynamically with God, open to the ever-renewed givenness of the world experienced as creation, responsive to the ever-new demands of life experienced as revelation, and devoted to the work of love in the world for the sake of redemption. The Bible is thus the ongoing record of the concrete life of Israel in relationship with God and illustrates the profound truths of religious revelation as it makes claims upon persons and the community. Thus, Rosenzweig argued, the ancient Israelite, like the Jew of yesteryear or today, when faced with the immediacy of God's presence, did not experience the demands presented at the moment as external laws imposed from without. They were rather experienced as immediate commandments, as tasks that must be done for the sake of integrity and truth. This, he claimed, is the living religious source of the commandments in the Bible and in Judaism, for they are dynamic translations into human terms of the experience of God's loving presence. For this reason, tradition, which is the community's record of its attempts to "institutionalize" these moments of divine-human meeting and extend their reality into human life, is a valuable vessel of the sacred. Naturally, through overuse or abuse, the forms of tradition may lose their immediate impact and religious vitality. And so it may become necessary from time to time for religious individuals and alienated Jews alike to reexperience them afresh as powerful vehicles of an engaged religious life.

For a modern Jew, this appropriation of the ancient tradition as the bearer of authentic religious expressions may be extremely difficult. Indeed, Rosenzweig's close friend, Martin Buber, could not make the move toward a God who gave laws. Rosenzweig felt that Buber misunderstood or chose not to understand the issue. As for himself, Rosenzweig was willing to risk seeing the laws of tradition as potential commandments, but he realized that this willingness, or readiness, was only the beginning. The reappropriation of Judaism by the modern Jew could not be done at once, he said, or without honest struggle, for the modern Jew is neither simply a believer who accepts the *halakha* nor simply an unbeliever who rejects it; he or she accepts and rejects at once, responding to the demands of tradition with the sensibilities of his or her own life and thought. In this attitude, Rosenzweig reflects his unique stance in modern Jewish thought. Like the perspective of Orthodoxy, he accepted the objective givenness and authority of the tradition; but he did not accept it as an absolute or necessary truth for himself until he lived it part by part. And like the attitude of religious liberalism, Rosenzweig accepted the importance of subjective choice in the ritual expression of one's religious life; but he also did not accept the arbitrary assumption that certain traditions are either antiquated or sterile *until they are experienced and lived.* Thus, he argued, one must start with life, with a positive decision to *live Jewishly.* For the assimilated or alienated Jew of his time, Rosenzweig's words and personal example were a provocation all the more challenging for the honesty they assumed and demanded. Nothing modern had to be rejected; no sense of individual freedom, no secular knowledge, and no life experience had to be foregone. On the contrary, all this and more was to brought to the service of one's Jewish life. Only in this way, he felt, would Judaism be revived as a vital religious expression.

In the years that followed the war, Rosenzweig made some decisive personal decisions and actualized his visions in institutional form. He realized that an important carrier of the Jewish traditions and the bridge to its inner life and self-renewal was study. He established a model "school," the Freies Juedisches Lehrhaus in Frankfurt. The name was not fortuitous. As a "House of Jewish Study," Rosenzweig hoped to signal his distance from the dispassionate academic study of Judaism or, indeed, from any uninvolved intellectual accumulation of details. And he further hoped to recapture in a modern form the older style of "learning" of sacred texts in which what was studied was transformed into life. No texts were in principle excluded from the curriculum, and not all of the instructors in the Lehrhaus were "experts." The ideal was that teachers were also expected to learn and the students were also expected to teach; each was to give and receive reciprocally out of personal knowledge and experience. All that was required was the willingness to study the texts and bring them alive—in whatever way—in one's own life as vital forces. In this way a return to the sources would be a modern return to the roots of Jewish expression, where one could always learn and be instructed—provided that there was "readiness."

The Lehrhaus assembled among its teachers some of the more remarkable intellectual personalities of the time (including Martin Buber, Erich Fromm, Nahum Glatzer, Gershom Scholem, and Ernst Simon) and quickly became an adult education enterprise of enormous cultural significance. This went on for a number of years, at first under the direct supervision of Rosenzweig himself. After 1921, when he began to notice the effect of progressive paralysis, the immediate supervision of the Lehrhaus was taken over by colleagues and a new, more intimate Lehrhaus was formed in the privacy of Rosenzweig's apartment. Here, remarkably, with virtually no physical powers save eye movements, Rosenzweig carried on a voluminous correspondence, studied Jewish sources, especially the Talmud, translated and commented upon the religious poetry of Judah Halvei, and from 1923 on worked with Martin Buber on a new German translation of the Bible—one that cannot be read passively but must be engaged with the eye and ear "in life." (Ten volumes were jointly completed; the remainder were done by Buber alone over the next three decades.) As was traditional, this more private Lehrhaus, the "house of study," was also a "house of prayer" and Rosenzweig's friends conducted religious services for him over the years of his illness. Near the end (and not disclosed until after Rosenzweig's death), Leo Baeck, a liberal rabbi and theologian of great distinction (who refused to leave his people during the horrors of World War II and preserved for them the image of human dignity in the concentration camp of Theresianstadt), conferred upon Franz Rosenzweig the ancient rabbinical title of *moreynu*, "Our Teacher." For such he had become and would remain for many, his life and thought a new link in an ancient tradition and a testimony that Judaism could be revived as a vital reality for the complex but honest modern Jew.

Martin Buber (1878–1965), the close friend of Franz Rosenzweig and his collaborator in their joint Bible translation, walked a different path to Jewish commitment. Buber's early years were marked by an intimate awareness of authentic eastern European piety and of Maskil-like scholarship and also by a deep involvement in the aesthetics and attitudes of late nineteenth-century Europe. As a boy, he spent considerable time in Galicia on the estate of his grandfather, Salomon Buber, who in his spare time devoted himself to producing critical editions of midrashic works scattered throughout the world's libraries. This early contact with the nonhalakhic sources of the Jewish spiritual imagination impressed young Buber, as also did his trips to local Hasidic prayer houses. But Martin Buber was pulled in other directions. He became involved with the thinking of Nietzsche at an early age and studied Western philosophy and art history at various European universities. Though a nonpracticing Jew, Buber was nevertheless profoundly committed to the Jewish cultural renaissance of Zionism. His was an early and important voice for a nontraditional renewal of the spiritual resources of Jewish culture.

Buber's commitment to cultural Zionism took many forms. He was a serious advocate of the new agricultural settlements then being founded in the land of Israel (the *kibbutzim*), seeing in them important moral experiments in the renewing power of human community. In the 1930s Buber showed his true greatness in reviving the Lehrhaus and traveling throughout Germany in a heroic effort to teach the sources of Judaism to his beleaguered people and thus give them the cultural resources for a spiritual resistance to Fascism. After the war, Buber recognized that the task of rescuing the Jewish survivors of the death camps gave Herzl's program of political Zionism a special moral urgency. He nevertheless continued to speak out forcefully on behalf of cultural renewal in the State of Israel and tried to instill in the new refugees—many of whom had no previous Zionist training—his ideals of the creation of a new Jew, spiritually alert and proud, in touch with both a life of culture and a life on the earth.

Buber's concern for a broad cultural renewal led in many literary directions. He translated selections of Chinese folk tales, worked on the Finnish *Kalevala* epic, and wrote studies on Christian mysticism. At the same time, Buber began an intense study of Jewish religious sources, specifically those of Hasidism. Buber began a lifelong project of presenting these sources to ther world-at-large, beginning with books of the tales of the Ba'al Shem Tov and Rabbi Nahman of Bratzlav and especially through his celebrated *Tales of the Hasidim*. In these and other writings, he presented Hasidism as the direct inheritor of the authentic teachings of Judaism and rooted in the Bible. These teachings included alertness to the demands of the living God; a consecration of daily life through "sacramental living," where every deed was given the highest moral and religious significance; concern for the unity of life and the tyranny of idolatry; and the restorative power of a human community unified around these ideals. His goal in these works was not detached historical reconstruction but engaged living for the sake of cultural renewal. Herein lay Buber's practical goals of creating a new Jewish person, of forming a new posttraditional but spiritually enriched Jewish existence, and of saving culture from encrustation by reviving the heart and soul of persons.

Beyond these involvements, Buber was particularly influential through his great theological meditation *I and Thou* (1923). In this work, Buber avowedly turned away from the mystical self-absorptions of his youth and toward dialogical living, a living wherein all life is "meeting" and "relationship" with nature, persons, and God. Buber saw life as turning around two poles of relationship: the "I-It" pole, where relations are detached, manipulative, and move between a subject (the self) and an object (things or other persons), and the "I-Thou" pole, where relations are spontaneous, reciprocal, and involve one's total being. Naturally, all "I-It" relations are not bad, and some are even necessary for living. But if the "I-It" pole predominates in life, as Buber feared it had come to do in modern technological society, it tends to block out the possibility of intense sharing. In the "I-Thou" relation, one subject is deeply responsive to the presence and need of another subject, who, while experienced as an "other," is not experienced as an "object" and is not swallowed up in one's subjectivity. Rather, the other person remains a wholly present reality who can only be known through shared living. God, in truth, is the "Eternal Thou," says Buber, the Thou that can never be objectified and Who shines forth in true meetings between persons or between them and other aspects of reality. God, then, is the eternal, living Presence that can be responded to through individuals and nature or reduced to idolatrous and manipulated forms. To respond to the living reality as it appears before the self is to respond to God's Presence, his eternal revelation. To ignore this living reality because of private needs or contrivances is to sin, for it is to objectify reality or God out of fear or for the sake of power and self-interest. The human task, says Buber, is to make the world "God-real," to make the Presence of the Eternal Thou more and more active and present in the human community.

For Buber, the great Jewish texts of the Bible and Hasidism preserve these insights and, if one is open to them, may direct the alienated, self-absorbed, and fearful human soul of the modern era to their life-giving power. Here was a reinterpretation of classical sources that was no renewal of traditional Judaism per se, but a confidence in the truthfulness of parts of the Jewish tradition to renew Jewish life in unexpected and nonparochial ways. As observed earlier, Buber did not share Rosenzweig's belief that the commandments of Judaism were potential carriers of such religious renewal. He rather saw them as external constraints against responsiveness to the spiritual demands of the moment. It is for this reason, among others, that many modern Jewish traditionalists have found it difficult to appreciate aspects of Buber's teaching. But to dismiss Martin Buber as an inauthentic Jewish teacher because he was not traditionally observant is to err profoundly, for Buber's voice speaks out of the depths of Jewish religious sources—though for him the challenge of "Sinai" is everywhere and with no fixed form. Buber challenged the modern individual, and the Jew in particular, to live an authentic existence, one that demanded spiritual focus and integrity in every action and at every moment. In this Buber was one in his thought and life. Like the world of Simeon the Righteous of old, the world of Martin Buber also stood on three things: Torah study, committed service to the world, and good deeds. His model of choice and decision remains significant for contemporary Jews, in all their various forms of commitment to the Jewish religious tradition.

A Tale of Two Centers: Israel and the United States

Israel

The modern State of Israel is a major spiritual and spatial focus for contemporary Jewry. As the center of a renewed national life, its cultural and political achievements since 1948 are a source of pride for Jews the world over. Many make secular "pilgrimages" to the civil shrines of the new state—the communal farms (*kibbutzim*), the parliament (Knesset), the development towns in the desert, and the Holocaust memorials (like Yad Va-Shem)—and spend time studying at its universities or just touring the land. Many others come to Israel with specifically religious goals in mind, though the two motivations are not mutually exclusive. Among the religious purposes for travel to Israel is the trend for American youngsters to celebrate a *bar mitzvah* at the old Temple wall (the Wailing Wall) in Jerusalem, for Orthodox high-school students to spend a year in a *yeshiva*, and for all Jews to participate in its diverse and intense synagogue life. The existence in Israel of thousands of prayer rooms and synagogues, where the customs of Jews from Poland to Bukhara are actively practiced, imbues the visitor with wonder at the range of traditional Jewish culture and its many modes of modern expression. Being a virtual microcosm of Jewish diversity and commonality over the ages, the religious life in Israel thus often inspires new commitments to Jewish identity. And being itself a virtual microcosm of Jewish cultural creativity over the ages, the very land of Israel, with its archeological ruins and Byzantine ramparts, inspires reflections on Jewish history and the imperatives of continuity. No matter how traditional or secular the individual, all these activities are interpreted by modern Jews in religious terms, and the feelings evoked by them are understood as religious experiences. However paradoxical to the outsider, this is a basic fact of contemporary Jewish life—a modern expression of Judaism as a national-religious culture.

Within Israel itself, the diversity of religious life must be seen as a more complex affair, for while there is a polar split between the traditionalists and the secularists, the traditionalist group covers a volatile range from the modern to the ultra-Orthodox. Thus, due to the politicization of religious interest groups and the increasing institutionalization of the chief rabbinate, certain areas of law have been given over to the Orthodox coalitions (e.g., control over personal law like marriage and divorce and in some cities control over public issues like the prohibition of public transportation and the closing of movie theaters on the Sabbath). Such restrictions have often seemed to secularists to compromise their civil liberties, and tensions occasionally erupt when the one group or the other lobbies to increase or consolidate its position (within or outside of the law). Because of the general inflexibility of the rabbinate to compromise on issues it believes to be divine law, the concern that even most secularists have that traditional *halakha* play a role in the development of a common law in the state is increasingly tested. The lack of separation between "religion" and "state" has thus turned religious versus secular values into political interests—a result that has left little room for a middle ground. There are thus very few expressions of liberal religion in Israel. And the few attempts in this direction have often been harassed by the strict traditionalists, from whom the liberals must receive political approval (and religious certifications); or they have been rejected by the secularists, who have become antagonistic to all religious groups and can hardly conceive of a nondogmatic form of traditionalism. Paradoxically, coalitions between traditionalists and secularists do occur when political or security interests are involved (though the often messianic motivation of the former will not be shared by the latter).

Among the traditionalists, there are great differences as well. In their common struggle against secularism, the various traditionalists are vitally concerned to determine the Jewish character of the state. The spectrum of traditionalism ranges from the modern Orthodox, whose lives are determined by *halakha* but who also promote the civic democratic concerns of a Western state, to the ultra-Orthodox, who either reject the state outright or wish to influence it by working politically for the totalization of halakhic norms in the public realm.

Since these positions involve strongly diverse feelings about the Jewish character of the state, about Western democracy and respect for the law, and (increasingly) about the messianic character of the times (i.e., whether the "return to Zion" is part of the divine fulfillment of ancient prophecies), strongly diverse behaviors are generated. At one time, the players in this drama and their attitudes were easily identified by how Western their clothes were, the nature and size of their headcovering, and whether the "Holy Tongue" of Hebrew was spoken in daily life or only in prayer. Today, many of these distinctions are harder to make, and extreme traditionalists include new immigrants from the West or young Israelis imbued with the passion "to increase Torah and to strengthen it."

Quite certainly, each group in the State of Israel feels a responsibility to mold the Jewish character of the country in its own image. The political compromise to separate education into traditional and secularist branches simply ensures the fact that each group is only exposed to its own values. Thus where traditionalists will lobby so that halakhic values will determine medical ethics (including such matters as abortion, autopsy, and genetic testing), secularists will often reject these positions on political grounds and not necessarily on the basis of the values involved. Similarly, secularist concerns for civil liberties and democratic values are often spurned by traditionalists because they are sponsored by nonbelievers and nonhalakhists. The struggles go on every day; so that the future character of Jewish life in the State of Israel can only be guessed at. The higher birthrate of the ultra-traditionalists and their development of committed voting blocs are viewed by them as positive indicators of eventual political predominance. Such developments evoke serious concern among the more liberal traditionalists and certainly among the completely secular Israeli Jews. The latter hope that the ancient ideal of the unity of the Jewish people will stimulate all to work for a conciliatory consensus.

The United States

If there is a concern among Jews in the State of Israel to find a unifying consensus to overcome their various political-religious polarizations, a concern for the cultural and physical survival of the Jewish people is the unifying consensus of Jews who enjoy a multifaceted political-religious pluralism in the United States. Founded on the principle of the separation of church and state, religious life in America has encouraged its diverse religious and ethnic constituencies to strengthen their respective communal positions. In the Jewish case, this has meant the development of regional and national federations that include religious *and* nonreligious interest groups. Since these federations are responsible for the whole (regional or national) Jewish community, a spirit of pluralism and conciliation has generally prevailed, even where the religious divisions have been quite marked. Moreover, since Jews have been an ethnic-religious minority, it has been important for them to remain unified to promote their interests at local and state levels, particularly in earlier decades when Jews were generally restricted from the use of certain medical or communal institutions and limited by (unofficial) quotas from enrollment in universities and acceptance in established gentile law or business firms. For these and other reasons, Jews in America have supported causes favoring participatory democracy and the role of small interest groups. Naturally, this has further affected its religious life. The acrimony once common in Europe between liberal and orthodox Jews has never been a common feature of Jewish life in America.

In the main, the immigrants to America from Europe and Russia in the nineteenth century determined its religious and communal patterns. Early waves of German Jews brought with them the Reform ideology developed by Geiger and others and thus promoted changes in the liturgy (e.g., abbreviated prayers, vernacular and responsive hymn singing, and mixed seating). A liberal attitude towards halakhic regulations was fostered: dietary and Sabbath rules were relaxed or abandoned and traditional headcoverings were rejected or made optional. Devotion to America led in the early years to the rejection of the Jews as a nation (and so of Zionism) and the promotion of universal brotherhood. The fact that the first Reform rabbinical seminary was established in Ohio symbolizes the general early American orientation toward the Midwest heartlands. In many respects, Reform Judaism introduced features of the Protestant style of religion into Judaism and often turned the rabbi from a scholar into a preacher, who sat on a raised dais in clerical garb facing the congregation. Moreover, a result of alienation from the tradition was that many congregants would simply live out their religious affiliation through the rabbi and see religion as a sometime Saturday (or Friday night) affair with little relation to one's values and habits the work week long. In recent years, Reform Judaism has become more traditionally minded, a vanguard for liturgical creativity within traditional categories, and a supporter of the State of Israel. In its concern for universal and social causes and outrage at civil abuses in the United States and abroad, Reform Judaism has helped keep the moral conscience of American Jewry.

Those Jews who later came to America from eastern Europe and Russia near and after the turn of the century brought with them the older traditional patterns and their modern compromises. Conservative Judaism, for example, is derivative of the more moderate reform groups in Europe—those who maintained strong links to traditional study and piety, though recognizing the historical character of Judaism. In America, the Conservatives have permitted some changes in the liturgy and *halakha*, but this has been done with great caution. Thus, while some Conservatives introduced occasional responsive reading in English into the service and permitted mixed seating, a strong respect for the dietary and Sabbath regulations remained, and the liturgy has remained traditional in both content and language. As has always been customary in traditional circles, the local Conservative rabbi (though now also in consultation with his "ritual committee" and under the moral guidance of a rabbinical committee of "law and standards" at the Conservative seminary) is in control of the religious practices of his congregation. The result is a broad spectrum of behaviors and beliefs among those Jews who are affiliated with Conservative congregations. This pluralistic temper remains the case even around such controversial issues as permitting congregants to drive to Sabbath or festival services (only), allowing women to be called up to bless the Torah in their own right, and permitting women to be hired or to officiate as rabbis. This last is a very new matter for Conservative Jews, since only in past years have women been accepted to its rabbinic school (the practice has been common in Reform seminaries for a decade and more).

Jews from eastern Europe also solidified the Orthodox community of America, which continued along traditional lines in matters of authority, practice, and education. Nevertheless, use of the public schools or secular studies was assumed. In the emergent "modern

Orthodox" style, as it has been called, firm roots in tradition are maintained and business involvements and social contacts in the wider gentile environment are accepted. Naturally, tensions arise over such compromises. But the "modern Orthodox" claim that their struggle for such integration is in the true spirit of tradition, which has always been open to the wider educational and economic world—though cautiously integrating these (or, at times, living in "two spheres"). The more traditional Orthodox in the United States, many of whom came as immigrants after World War II, generally resist contact with the secular world and live in isolated and self-imposed ghettos, where they claim they can authentically preserve the values and life patterns of a "Torah-true" Judaism. Jews in these spheres are largely restricted to traditional Jewish cultural patterns, and they have developed an intense and self-absorbed communal structure. For them, modernity is an outright blasphemy and threat to all that they hold sacred. These feelings are also related to their ideological concern for the soul of secular Jews and their attempts to convert these nonobservant coreligionists back to the true, traditional path.

Among the notable recent developments in modern Jewish life in America is the growth of day-school education, among the modern Orthodox and Conservative Jews especially. Such education integrates the serious study of classical Jewish sources along with the equally serious study of secular subjects, all within a framework where traditional values are lived. The day-school phenomenon reflects a new enhancement of traditional education among America's Jews and institutionalizes a new style of integrating Jewish and Western culture. According to their differing halakhic temperaments, the two religious movements promote the values and benefits of each. The further supplementation of day-school and afternoon (Hebrew school) education with intense Jewish summer camp experiences has also deepened the commitments of young Jews to Judaism and helped them to conceptualize and live models of Jewish identity that are thoroughly at home in the traditional culture and the secular ambience.

Patterns of adult education or study groups sponsored by synagogues try to foster greater Jewish knowledge among the older generations. Talmud study groups for men have always been customary in Orthodox settings, and some modern Orthodox have established

Celebration of Simhat Torah, *the Festival of Rejoicing over the Law. At the conclusion of the annual cycle of reading, all children are collectively "called up" to the Torah, and an honored adult recites the appropriate blessing. The children are standing under an outspread tallit—symbolic of the marriage canopy and the holy marriage (the covenant) between God and Israel. Photo credit: Bill Aron.*

Talmud classes for women as well. In Conservative and Reform circles, many of these study groups are also intense family fellowships (called *havurot*), which may meet for smaller prayer gatherings within the framework of the larger congregations. The "Havurah" movement has also promoted the organization of such small prayer-study communities in their own right. The style of prayer and adherence to tradition in these groups is determined by the members, and their nonhierarchical structure encourages egalitarian participation for men and women along with various types of liturgical innovations. In some ways, this movement transcends the ideologies of earlier American generations and, in its serious commitment to tradition in a style that is at once nondogmatic and concerned to reflect the values of its participants (typically liberal, self-expressive, and participatory), a new synthesis of tradition and modernity is being formed—something uniquely American.

It may be added that the full participation of women in these groups, in Reform congregations and increasingly in Conservative synagogues, is a structural change in traditional Jewish practice of the greatest moment. The full implications of this change cannot yet be gauged. One can only surmise that the full involvement of women within Jewish piety and study will have serious implications for a yet-to-emerge liberal-traditional sensibility. Certainly one of the upshots of the Havurah pattern and new feminine involvements in Judaism, whose impact can already be felt, is the growing sense that Jews must take active and creative responsibility for their own religious lives. Not for nothing have Franz Rosenzweig and Martin Buber been the spiritual godfathers for many of the intellectuals involved in these developments. Together with this, a new emphasis on the aggadic imagination—an imagination that cultivates religious wonder and the delight in traditional literary images—has given the old halakhic patterns a new vibrancy for such "heterodox" Jews. From a historical point of view, the emergence of new motivations for practicing the commandments has always signaled vitality and renewal in Judaism.

The shapes and expressions of Jewish life in Israel and the United States at the close of the twentieth century could hardly have been anticipated a century ago, and one may expect new syntheses and patterns in the future. The modern Jewish scholar and thinker, Simon Rawidowicz, once referred to Jews as the "ever-dying people", so precariously perched has Jewish civilization been on the twigs of alien trees. But Jews and Judaism are also being ever renewed and reborn—more so now than ever as Jews the world over have developed political power and a new will to determine their historical destiny. This new will and power has led to some fragmenting results, splitting Jewish groups among themselves. But it has also promoted new expressions of traditional practice and an unapologetic sense of national-religious vitality. Whether a new consensus can arise from this diversity will largely depend on the spirit of the Jews themselves. Certainly the basis for this new consensus is present in the calendrical cycle, which all Jews share in some way, as well as in the values of Torah, *halakha*, and peoplehood—no matter how diversely interpreted and implemented. Moreover, though the Jewish tradition has fostered dogmatic as well as nondogmatic trends and both flexible and inflexible constructions of its laws, what often determined which trend or construction was emphasized were a series of meta-halakhic values. Chief among these values are equity, loving-kindness, and *ahavat Yisrael*, "love of the people of Israel." Many Jews today believe that the role of these values will greatly determine the fate of the old-new religion of Judaism in the years to come.

Notes

1. Babylonian Talmud, *Menahot* 29b.

2. The text occurs in the edition of *Sefer Hasidim (Das Buch der Frommen)* of J. Wistinetzki (Berlin: Itzkowski, 1891), p. 6.

3. Babylonian Talmud, *Baba Metzia* 59b.

4. *Mishnah Shevi'ith* X. 3–4.

5. *Mishnah Nezikin* I. 2 (*Ethics of the Fathers*). See *The Ethics of the Talmud: Sayings of the Fathers,* ed. and trans. R. T. Herford (New York: Schocken, 1966), p. 22.

6. See *The Authorized Daily Prayer Book,* ed. J. Hertz (New York: Bloch Publishing Company, 1955), p.149.

7. *Avot de-Rabbi Nathan,* ed S. Schechter (New York: Feldheim, 1967), version A, chap. 4, p. 21. (See *The Fathers According to Rabbi Nathan,* trans. J. Goldin (Yale Judaica Series X; New Haven: Yale University Press, 1955), p. 34.

8. From "Lord, Where Shall I Find You?" Complete text in *The Penguin Book of Hebrew Verse,* ed. and trans. T. Carmi (New York: Penguin, 1981), pp. 338–339.

9. See "Ode to Zion" in ibid., p. 347.

10. *The Guide of the Perplexed,* trans. S. Pines (Chicago: University of Chicago Press, 1963), pp. 11–12.

11. Ibid., p. 622.

12. Ibid.

13. *Kuzari* III. 65.

14. *Zohar* II. 99 a–b. See translation of D. Matt (New York, Paulist Press, 1983), pp. 121–123.

Glossary*

Akiba. Distinguished rabbi in ancient Palestine (c. 50–135 C.E.). A major legal scholar, who established an academy in Bne Brak, Akiba ben Joseph was also a legendary mystic and martyr. He was tortured and killed by the Romans in 135 C.E.

Ashkenazi. Originally the designation *Ashkenaz* referred to a people and country bordering on Armenia and the upper Euphrates; in medieval times, it referred to the Jewish area of settlement in northwest Europe. The whole cultural complex deriving from this region is known as Ashkenazi; hence it now refers to Jews of European and Russian background and their distinctive liturgical practices or religious and social customs. The term is in contradistinction to Sephardi.

ben. "Son," "son of" in Hebrew; Rabbi Akiba ben Joseph means Akiba son of Joseph.

bar (bat) mitzvah. Literally, "son (daughter)-of-the-commandment(s)." The phrase originally referred to a person responsible for performing the divine commandments of Judaism; it now refers to the occasion when a boy or girl reaches the age of religious majority and responsibility (thirteen years for a boy; twelve years and a day for a girl).

circumcision. The minor surgical removal of the foreskin when a Jewish boy is eight days old. The ceremony is called *brit milah,* which indicates that the ritual establishes a covenant between God and the individual.

commandments. According to rabbinic tradition, there are 613 religious commandments referred to in the Torah (and elaborated upon by the rabbinic sages). Of these, 248 are positive commandments and 365 are negative. The numbers respectively symbolize the fact that divine service must be expressed through all one's bodily parts during all the days of the year. In Hebrew, the commandments are called *mitzvot* (sing., *mitzvah*). More ge-

---

*Prepared with the assistance of Eitan Fishbane.

nerically, a *mitzvah* refers to any act of religious duty or obligation; more colloquially, a *mitzvah* refers to a "good deed."

covenant. In the Bible, it refers to the religious bond between God and Israel contracted at Sinai with the giving of the Torah. For Judaism, it refers to the eternal bond between God and the people of Israel grounded in the nation's obedience to the divine commandments. It is a major theological concept, expressive of divine grace and concern for the Jews and their reciprocal obligations to God.

galut. Literally, "exile." The term refers to the various expulsions of Jews from the ancestral homeland. Over time, it came to express the broader notion of Jewish homelessness and state of being aliens. Thus, colloquially, "to be in *galut*" means to live in the Diaspora and also to be in a state of physical and even spiritual alienation.

halakha. Any normative Jewish law, custom, or practice—or the entire complex. *Halakha* is law established or custom ratified by authoritative rabbinic jurists and teachers. Colloquially, if something is deemed halakhic, it is considered proper and normative behavior.

Hillel. Often called by the title "the Elder." Probably a Babylonian, Hillel was an important sage of the classical period. He lived ca. 50 B.C.E.–ca. first century C.E. His teachings convey the Pharisaic ideal, through many epigrams on humility and peace (found in *Ethics of the Fathers,* chaps. 1–2); and were fundamental in shaping the Pharisaic traditions and modes of interpretation. In rabbinic lore, Hillel is famous for a negative formulation of the Golden Rule (recited to a heathen): "What is hateful to you do not do to your fellow man. That is the whole Torah, the rest is commentary. Go and learn it." His style of legal reasoning is continued by his disciples, known as Beit Hillel ("House/ School of Hillel"), and is typically contrasted with that of Shammai (a contemporary) and his school.

Israel. In biblical times, this refers to the northern tribes, but also to the entire nation. Historically, Jews have continued to regard themselves as the true continuation of the ancient Israelite national-religious community. The term thus has a strong cultural sense. In modern times, it also refers to the political State of Israel.

Kaddish. Prayer recited by mourners for the dead. The prayer extols God's majesty and kingdom. There is also a version of the prayer recited by the prayer leader between major units of the public liturgy and a long version (called Rabbinic Kaddish) that follows an act of study. Most of the Kaddish is in Aramaic.

kosher. Literally, "proper," or "ritually permitted" food. Traditional Jewish dietary laws are based on biblical legislation. Only land animals that chew the cud and have cloven hoofs are permitted and must be slaughtered in a special way. Further, meat products may not be eaten with milk products or immediately thereafter. Only sea creatures (fish) having fins and scales are permitted. Fowl is considered a meat food and also has to be slaughtered in a special manner.

Maimonides. Major medieval rabbi, physician, scientist, and philosopher (1135–1204), known by the acronym Rambam. Born in Spain, Maimonides fled from persecution to Morocco and finally settled in Egypt. His major works include a legal commentary on the Mishnah, a law code called *Mishnah Torah,* and the preeminent work of medieval Jewish rational philosophy, *The Guide of the Perplexed.*

messiah. Literally, "anointed one." Based on an old biblical belief that a descendant of King David (a royal "anointed one") would establish an era of peace and justice for the nation of Israel and the world, expectations of a universal or cosmic redeemer developed in classical Judaism and were further refined and developed over the centuries. The messianic age was believed by some Jews to be a time of perfection of human institutions; others believed it to be a time of radical new beginnings, a new heaven and earth, after divine judgment and destruction. The period known as "days of messiah" may thus refer to this period of renewal, and not necessarily to an individual who inaugurates or rules the time.

mezuzah. Literally, "doorpost"; the scroll and container affixed by Jews to the exterior doorposts (at the right side of the entrance) of their home. By custom, interior doorways are also often marked by a *mezuzah*. The practice of affixing a *mezuzah* is based on a biblical passage (Deut. 6:1–4).

midrash. Literally, "exposition" or "inquiry" into the language, ideas, and narratives of the Torah. It constitutes a major literary achievement of classical and later Judaism. Its two major divisions are legal *midrash* (or *midrash halakha*) and nonlegal *midrash* (or *midrash aggadah;* this includes grammatical explications, theology, ethics, and legends).

Moses. The great biblical personality (c. thirteenth century B.C.E.) who led the nation out of Egyptian bondage and taught them the divine laws at Sinai. He is also presented as first of the prophets. Throughout Jewish history he is the exalted man of faith and leadership without peer.

Mishnah. Ancient code of Jewish law collated, edited, and revised by Rabbi Judah the Prince at the beginning of the third century C.E. The code is divided into six major units and sixty-three minor ones. The work is the authoritative legal tradition of the early sages and is the basis of the legal discussions of the Talmud.

mitzvot. See commandments.

Passover. Spring holiday celebrating the Exodus of the ancient Israelites from Egypt. The festival lasts eight days, during which Jews refrain from eating all leavened foods and products. A special ritual meal (called *seder*) is prepared, and a traditional narrative (called the *Haggadah*), supplemented by hymns and songs, marks the event.

rabbi. Hebrew, "My Master," an authorized teacher of the Jewish tradition. The role of the rabbi has changed considerably throughout the centuries. Traditionally, rabbis serve as the legal and spiritual guides of their congregations and communities. The title is conferred after considerable study of traditional Jewish sources. This conferral and its responsibilities is central to the chain of tradition in Judaism.

Rashi. Acronym for Rabbi Solomon ben Isaac (1040–1105), a great medieval sage of Troyes, France. He is the author of fundamental commentaries on the Talmud, and one of the most beloved and influential commentaries on the Bible. Characterized by great lucidity and pedagogy, his comments emphasized the plain, straightforward sense of a text.

Sabbath. The seventh day of the week (Heb., *shabbat*), recalling the completion of the creation and the Exodus from Egypt. It is a day symbolic of new beginnings and one dedicated to God, a most holy day of rest. The commandment of rest is found in the Bible and has been elaborated by the rabbis. It is a special duty to study Torah on the Sabbath and to be joyful. Sabbaths near major festivals are known by special names.

seder. The traditional service for holiday of Passover, which includes special food symbols and narratives. The order of the service is highly regulated (*seder* means "order"), and the traditional narrative is known as the *Haggadah*.

Sephardi. The designation *Sepharad* in biblical times refers to a colony of exiles from Jerusalem, possibly in or near Sardis; in medieval period, Sephardi Jews are those descended from those who lived in Spain and Portugal before the expulsion of 1492. As a cultural designation, the term refers to the cultural complex associated with Jews of this region and its related Diaspora in the Balkans and Middle East. The term is used in contradistinction to *Ashkenazi,* but it does not refer, thereby, to all Jews of non-Ashkenazi origin.

shema. Title of the fundamental, monotheistic statement of Judaism, found in Deut. 6:4 ("Hear, O Israel, the Lord is our God, the Lord is One"). This statement avers the unity of God, and is recited daily in the liturgy (along with Deut. 6:5–9, and other passages), and customarily before sleep at night. This proclamation also climaxes special liturgies (like Yom Kippur), and is central to the confessional before death and the ritual of martyrdom. The *Shema* is inscried on the *mezuzah* and the *tefillin*. In public services, it is recited in unison.

synagogue. The central insitution of Jewish communal worship and study since antiquity. The structure of the building has changed, though in all cases the ark containing the Torah scrolls faces the ancient Temple site in Jerusalem.

tallit. A large shawl with fringes and special knots at the extremities, worn during morning prayers. The fringes, according to the

Bible, remind the worshiper of God's commandments. It is traditional for the male to be buried in his *tallit,* but without its fringes.

Talmud. Literally, "learning" or "study," the word is primarily used to refer to the classical rabbinic discussions of the Mishnah. These discussions are also known as *gemara;* and this has become a colloquial, generic terms for the *Talmud* and its study. There is a Babylonian Talmud and a Jerusalem Talmud. The first was completed in the fifth century C.E.; the second, also known as the Palestinian Talmud, was edited in the early fourth century C.E.

tefillin. The two black boxes containing scriptural citation worn by men and boys (of majority age) during morning services, though not on Sabbath and festivals. The *tefillin,* also called phylacteries, have leather thongs attached. One box (with four sections) is placed on the head, the other (with one section) is placed (customarily) on the left arm, near the heart. The biblical passages emphasize the unity of God and the duty to love God and be mindful of him with "all one's heart and mind."

Torah. The first five books of the Bible, also known as the Five Books of Moses, or the Pentateuch. The Torah, literally "instruction," is commonly used to refer to the entire range of Jewish teachings and practices.

Zion, Zionism. *Zion* is the ancient name for Jerusalem, but already in biblical times it served to indicate the national homeland. In this latter sense it served as a focus for Jewish national-religious hopes of renewal over the centuries. Ancient hopes and attachments to Zion gave rise to Zionist longings and movements since antiquity, culminating in the modern national liberation movement of that name. The Zionist cause helped the Jews return to Palestine in this century and found the State of Israel in 1948. The goal of Zionism is the political and spiritual renewal of the Jewish people in its ancestral homeland.

Selected Reading List

Classical Sources in Translation

Birnbaum, P., ed. *High Holiday Prayer Book*. New York: Hebrew Publishing Company, 1951.

Buber, M. *Tales of the Hasidim*. 2 vols. New York: Schocken, 1947–1948.

Carmi, T., ed. *The Penguin Book of Hebrew Verse*. New York: Penguin Books, 1981.

Danby, H., ed. *The Mishnah*. Oxford: Oxford University Press, 1933.

Epstein, I., ed. *The Babylonian Talmud*. 6 vols. London: Soncino, 1935–1952.

Freedman, H., ed. *The Midrash*. 10 vols. London: Soncino, 1939.

Ginzberg, L. *Legends of the Jews*. 7 vols. Philadelphia: Jewish Publication Society, 1909–38.

Glatzer, N., ed. *In Time and Eternity: A Jewish Reader*. New York: Schocken, 1961.

―――. *Language of Faith*. New York: Schocken, 1947.

Hertz, J., ed. *The Authorized Daily Prayer Book*. New York: Bloch Publishing Company, 1955.

―――. The Pentatuch and Haftorahs. London: Soncino, 1965.

Matt, D., trans. *Zohar: The Book of Enlightenment*. New York: Paulist Press, 1983.

Montefiore, C. G. & Loewe, H. J. eds. *A Rabbinic Anthology*. London: MacMillan, 193p.

Sperling, H., and M. Simon, trans. *The Zohar*. 5 vols. London: Soncino, 1931–1934.

Surveys and Topics in Jewish History and Thought
with Full Bibliographies

Baron, S. *A Social and Religious History of the Jews*. 16 vols. New York: Columbia University Press, 1952–.

Cohen, A., and P. Mendes-Flohr, eds. *Contemporary Jewish Religious*

Thought. New York: Scribner, 1987.

Encyclopedia Judaica. 16 vols. and suppl. 1971.

Guttman, J. *Philosophies of Judaism.* New York: Holt, Rinehart & Winston, 1964.

Green, A., ed. *Jewish Spirituality from the Bible Through the Middle Ages.* Vol. 1. New York: Crossroad, 1986.

Finkelstein, L., ed. *The Jews: Their History, Culture and Religion.* 2 vols. New York: Harper & Brothers, 1949.

Moore, G. F. *Judaism in the First Centuries of the Christian Era.* 2 vols. Cambridge, Mass.: Harvard University Press, 1927.

Scholem, G. *Major Trends in Jewish Mysticism.* New York: Schocken, 1956.

―――. *The Messianic Idea in Judaism.* New York: Schocken, 1971.